T0286176

PRAISE FOR KYLE GRAY

"Kyle Gray is an incredibly talented medium and guide for a new generation of spiritual seekers and the already converted."

GABRIELLE BERNSTEIN, BESTSELLING AUTHOR OF
MIRACLES NOW AND *THE UNIVERSE HAS YOUR BACK*

"Kyle Gray is now an expert on celestial connections and has the following to prove it."

YOU MAGAZINE

"I adore Kyle Gray. He helps you to reconnect with all that is wanting to rise up within you, be available to the benevolent support that already surrounds you and release what is wanting to fall away with grace and ease. Who doesn't want some of that?!"

REBECCA CAMPBELL, AUTHOR OF *LIGHT IS THE NEW BLACK* AND *RISE SISTER RISE*

"The hottest name in spirituality!"

SOUL & SPIRIT MAGAZINE

"I had full-bodied chills. Kyle Gray is the hottest, hippest medium who translates the wisdom of the angels in the most loving and relatable way possible. I couldn't recommend his brilliant spiritual gifts more."

MEGGAN WATTERSON, AUTHOR OF *MARY MAGDALENE REVEALED*
AND *HOW TO LOVE YOURSELF (AND SOMETIMES OTHER PEOPLE)*

"Kyle Gray is now one of the most successful 'angel readers' in the UK."

PSYCHOLOGIES MAGAZINE

"Kyle Gray is a natural down-to-earth psychic, I found him to be startlingly accurate. He has a remarkable spiritual connection."

DAVID R. HAMILTON PhD, AUTHOR OF *THE LITTLE BOOK OF KINDNESS*

"Kyle Gray has taught angel prayers to non-believers, absolute skeptics and people who have prayed in a certain fixed way for many years, with astounding results. Here he explains his dynamic methods of raising prayer to an inspired spiritual level where it hits the mark."

CYGNUS REVIEW

DIVINE MASTERS, ANCIENT WISDOM

ALSO BY KYLE GRAY

Books

Angel Numbers
Angel Prayers
Connecting with the Angels Made Easy
Light Warrior
Raise Your Vibration
Wings of Forgiveness
Angels Whisper in My Ear

Audiobooks

Light Warrior
Raise Your Vibration
Angel Prayer Meditations

Oracle Card Decks

The Angel Guide Oracle
Angels and Ancestors Oracle Cards
Keepers of the Light Oracle Cards
Angel Prayers Oracle Cards

Online Courses

Certified Angel Guide
Connecting with the Angels Made Easy

DIVINE MASTERS, ANCIENT WISDOM

Activations to Connect with Universal Spiritual Guides

KYLE GRAY

HAY HOUSE

Carlsbad, California • New York City
London • Sydney • New Delhi

Published in the United Kingdom by:
Hay House UK Ltd, The Sixth Floor, Watson House,
54 Baker Street, London W1U 7BU
Tel: +44 (0)20 3927 7290; Fax: +44 (0)20 3927 7291; www.hayhouse.co.uk

Published in the United States of America by:
Hay House Inc., PO Box 5100, Carlsbad, CA 92018-5100
Tel: (1) 760 431 7695 or (800) 654 5126
Fax: (1) 760 431 6948 or (800) 650 5115; www.hayhouse.com

Published in Australia by:
Hay House Australia Pty. Ltd, 18/36 Ralph St, Alexandria NSW 2015
Tel: (61) 2 9669 4299; Fax: (61) 2 9669 4144; www.hayhouse.com.au

Published in India by:
Hay House Publishers India, Muskaan Complex,
Plot No.3, B-2, Vasant Kunj, New Delhi 110 070
Tel: (91) 11 4176 1620; Fax: (91) 11 4176 1630; www.hayhouse.co.in

A catalogue record for this book is available from the British Library.

Hardcover ISBN: 978-1-78817-515-9
E-book ISBN: 978-1-78817-544-9
Audiobook ISBN: 978-1-78817-601-9

Interior illustrations: 48: alexciopata/123RF; 49: Dmitry Rogatnev/123RF
51: Shutterstock/Marzz Studio

10 9 8 7 6 5 4 3 2 1

Printed in the United States of America

It is my prayer that I have done this subject justice. Ancient wisdom traditions have been a lifelong interest of mine and deciding which masters and deities to include in this space has taken months of work and preparation. I have aimed to take a balanced approach. There are many incredible keepers of ancient wisdom out there and it's my prayer that the 33 that I have chosen to include here will support your journey and enrich your life.

It is extremely important to me to respect traditions. I acknowledge that some of the deities included in this book are connected to traditions into which I am not initiated. It is for this reason alone that I have shared my own perspective and experiences, while trying to remain respectful of the ideas shared about these beings in all the traditions to which they are connected.

I know that there are many roads to experiencing love and the Source of creation. I pray that with this book I have opened doorways to experiences of love and connection, and that I have done so in a way that honors and respects the Divine Masters.

I am grateful for all that I have learnt along the way and for all of the personal experiences that have unfolded while I have been writing this book.

May it support the activation of the ancient wisdom that resides within you.

CONTENTS

LIST OF ACTIVATIONS

INTRODUCTION

You can't get far in most spiritual classes, workshops, or trainings in the West today without at least one of the Ascended Masters being introduced, or being present in the form of a statue on an altar or an image on a wall. Also known as the Masters of Ancient Wisdom, and as Divine Masters here, they are a congregation of enlightened beings, spiritual guides, and souls who have dedicated their energy and intelligence to the healing and nurturing of the world.

It is believed that these beings are universal spiritual guides who are operating on a multi-dimensional level, meaning that they are not limited to linear time and space and that anyone can connect and work with them, just as they can with angels.

Ascended Masters have appeared in different spiritual traditions with different names, but similar roles, teachings, and even locations. For example, Buddhists have believed that Ascended Masters reside in Shambhala, a city hidden in the Himalayas, while many *sadhus*, the wandering men of India, have spoken of hidden temples, and Christian traditions have taught that there is a Communion of Saints, a gathering of human souls and angels in heaven.

I was first introduced to the term "Ascended Masters" in my teenage years. It was around the time I was beginning to learn crystal therapy and energy healing, and I remember my Reiki teacher, Avril, who had become a real mentor, speaking about how helpful it was to have a spiritual being or guide you could call on to help you on your journey. You didn't have to have had personal experience of that being, but could call on one you were drawn to, either because of their story or what they stood for.

I remember asking for examples and Avril telling me about her special connection to Quan Yin, a female buddha and goddess figure representing divine compassion and utter acceptance. I liked the feeling that came to me as she spoke.

Then she pointed to a little altar by her bay window with a large porcelain statue of an oriental woman standing on top of a lotus.

"There's a statue of her there," she said.

Amazing. I was covered in goosebumps.

"I'll be calling her in when I give you your Reiki attunement today."

I felt warm and fuzzy.

And so my journey to the masters began…

It led me down a rabbit hole of spiritual practice and research. I bought every book on the subject that I could find, digging deep into esoteric teachings from the Western Mystery Tradition and looking into everything from secret societies such as the Golden Dawn to the challenging writings of Helena P. Blavatsky and discourses of Alice Bailey.

I've learnt a lot, but what I've come to understand over the last 17 years is that there's nothing more powerful than personal experience. That's why I want to help you make your own connection to these incredible spiritual allies.

PART I

INTRODUCING
THE MASTERS

Divine Source of creation,

I align my intentions with the highest good.

The light of the universe surrounds me with
the highest form of protection.

I am safe in my body and being,

Surrounded by angels of light.

I am ready to embark upon a spiritual journey.

I am ready to deepen my awareness and
heighten my spiritual connection.

Thank you, great teacher within, for leading the way.

The power of the cosmos exists within me.

I am led by the light of stars.

I am aligned with the highest good and the highest truth.

And so it is.

CHAPTER 1

WHO ARE THE MASTERS?

"As above, so below."

THE EMERALD TABLET

Traditionally, the Ascended Masters, or Mahatmas, as they were originally called when they were first introduced in the Theosophical teachings of the late 1800s, are beings who have walked the Earth before us and are now able to offer divine intelligence and support on a spiritual level. Jesus and the Buddha are great examples. Although they are connected to two of the world's major religions, they go beyond the limitations of religion, and many people the world over feel connected to their power, presence, and energy.

The original masters in Theosophy didn't include previously known spiritual figures such as Jesus and the Buddha, but over the years the ideas, connections, and experiences that have been added to the "Ascended Master teachings" have transcended specific traditions and become more universal in nature.

Personally, I feel that anyone who has made a remarkable difference to the planet, either through social activism, exceptional leadership, or sharing their gifts, is an Ascended Master. Highly influential souls such as Martin Luther King Jr., Bob Marley, and Mother Teresa are all great examples. I genuinely believe that we all have Ascended Masters in our own family lineage. We may have had a great-grandparent who did something extremely brave or survived extraordinarily difficult conditions. Whoever they may be, we can connect with the spirit and intelligence of the Ascended Masters and benefit from their wisdom and guidance.

Many of the Ascended Masters in this book surmounted extremely challenging circumstances in a human life. It's because of how they overcame these challenges that they are able to offer an "enlightened" perspective from the higher realms.

Deities, Masters, and Light Beings

Information about the masters differs slightly from teacher to teacher. It was never clear in the original writings, for example, if the masters were still on the Earth as enlightened beings who were communicating telepathically or were spiritual guides who were connecting through some sort of spirit communication. I think it's important to acknowledge that all spiritual matters are very personal in nature and to find the path or idea that best resonates with your own energy and truth. I've also come to understand that every medium or spiritual teacher shares their work through their perspective, or what I like to call "filter." Which is fine, because it's their truth.

When I was doing research ahead of writing this book, my intention was to really go deep down the rabbit hole of the traditional Ascended Master teachings and the teachings of Theosophy. After spending some time in meditation and connection over this, though, I felt that I needed to provide a broader range of Ascended Masters and include deities and other light beings.

One major issue that came to light while I was refreshing my knowledge of the traditional masters in Theosophy, such as El Morya, Kuthumi, Saint Germain, and Djwal Khul, was the extreme lack of feminine energy. I realized that although the Ascended Masters had brought something new, something beyond mainstream religion, their presentation had been affected deeply by the patriarchal system of the time. There was a reason for this. Helena Blavatsky, who was one of the founding teachers of Theosophy and the Ascended Master movement, was asexual, most likely because she was pressured into marriage at 17. Because of this disconnection from her feminine energy, she was apparently repulsed by women and sexuality. This filter affected her teachings, which didn't have an enlightened perspective on women. My truth does.

This patriarchal energy continued into the "I AM" Activity, a 20th-century spiritual movement that was clearly influenced by Blavatsky. Teachers in this movement were, I guess, either Christians, recovering Christians, or bringing Christian concepts into their teachings to make them more palatable for the Christian society that they were living in. You can see this clearly in their texts, especially the prayers to the masters.

I think it's important to understand that we all have the capacity to share spiritual teachings and we'll all do it through our own filters. This is the beauty of being human—we are all having our own experience and sharing from that space.

When I opened up on social media about writing a book on the masters, I asked which beings people felt connected to and worked with, and I wasn't surprised that a lot of those who replied included deities. So, this book draws together goddesses, gods, holy figures, New Age figures, and light beings. I have refrained from including archangels simply because I have written about angelic beings extensively elsewhere and this creates more space for me to cover some of the other amazing beings in the cosmos.

This book is a list of who's who in heaven, but that doesn't end here. I've put together a collection of beings I've learnt about and worked with on my journey, but if there's information that doesn't resonate with you, or differs from what you've heard or learnt elsewhere, or you feel someone important has been left out, please know that this is okay. I encourage you to delve deep into your own heart and connect with the truth that works best for you.

Universal Spiritual Guides

It's important to say that the Divine Masters are for *everyone*. Individual masters may have once been connected to a particular path or tradition, but they are all now transcending all limitations, including time and space. They are universal spiritual guides who can be called on anytime and anywhere, by anybody. We can all have our very own personal experience of them.

Having said that, there are a few general points to bear in mind. It's important to approach all of these beings with utmost respect, knowing that the spark of Source exists within them all. Each deity or god is ultimately an aspect of God. Then there are the avatars of the Eastern traditions. *Avatar* means "descent," so is basically another term for physical incarnation. An avatar is a master or deity who has descended into a bodily vehicle to bring an embodiment of Source to the world.

Sacred Embodiments of Source

As someone who has spent time living on an ashram in India, I would also like to present a few physical guidelines for your consideration. Again, respect is key. Never put an image or statue of a deity on the floor, unless it is elevated in some way. For example, you'll see statues of the Buddha sitting on a block of some description, so that he's elevated. Also, always keep these sacred items clean. Respect them as you would a living deity who was in your home.

Another thing to keep in mind is your use of a sacred image. If someone who is connected to that particular lineage gives you feedback that your use is disrespectful or offensive, don't be offended by the feedback, just do all you can to improve the situation, because we both know offence was never your intention.

This brings us to another important point: intention is everything.

Our intention ultimately is what we hold deep within our heart. It's what the universe is listening for and responding to. Aligning with the highest intention will always support us in connecting to spiritual energy. If connecting on a spiritual level is new territory for you, your intention is what will lead you on this expedition, and it's also what will keep you aligned and protect your energy.

I think it's important here to assure you right at the outset that there's nothing to be worried about in making this connection. When I say "protect your energy," I'm not speaking about protecting yourself from things going wrong, just making you aware that when you open up on a spiritual level, it increases your sensitivity to the energies of the Earth and everything that's going on down here. I have created a whole section on energy protection (*p.71*), so that your journeys, activations, and connections with the divine realms are pleasurable.

Here are some important points to know in the meantime:

- You are powerful.
- You are the keeper of your mind and body.
- Wherever love is present, fear is a stranger.
- Love is within you.
- You are love.
- Connecting on a spiritual level is an adventure.
- You have angels all around you, leading the way.
- Your spirit is as loud as your willingness to listen. Be willing to listen.
- You always have a choice.
- Nothing can enter your field uninvited.
- You are safe.

CHAPTER 2

THE HISTORY OF THE MASTERS

"There is no higher religion than the truth."

HELENA P. BLAVATSKY

What I love most about the Ascended Master teachings is the strong connections they have with Eastern philosophy, in particular the Indo-Tibetan traditions such as Hinduism and Buddhism. I've been interested in both of these traditions since high school. In fact I would go as far as to say that my high-school religious studies teachers were some of the most influential spiritual teachers I've ever had.

I had a particularly strong connection with the head of the religious studies department, Mrs. B. I think initially it was because she loved my big cousin in high school, who was also a very keen student. It wasn't until she saw me reading a book on spiritual laws that our relationship began to develop, but soon she had introduced me to Eastern philosophy, and I've never looked back.

Mrs. B. was a fun teacher. She would tell us about an idea and then open it up to group discussion. This felt healthy to me and I always had something to say. I enjoyed learning about Rama and Sita from the Hindu tradition, though at the time I never imagined those personifications of the divine would become a whole teaching theme in the yoga classes I would give one day.

Mrs. B. herself may have been a Buddhist. I remember one day she was wearing a top that exposed her neck, and there, hanging from a gold chain, was a small figure of Gautama Buddha.

I told Mrs. B. about my interest in angels, spiritual law, Ascended Masters, and everything in between. We would meet during free periods and I would read my angel cards for her, which she absolutely loved.

She also led meditations in class and even hosted Amnesty International gatherings and another meditation class during the lunch break. She was truly inspirational, but one day she announced she was retiring and a new head of department was replacing her. Sadly, out of my whole year (nearly 200 students), I was one of only two who applied for the higher module in religious studies, and because of the lack of interest, the school refused to run the course. This was one of my many reasons for leaving school early. I had envisioned myself going on to become a religious studies teacher one day. I guess in a way that's kind of worked out, though. Back in high school I also had dreams of visiting India and since then my spiritual journey has taken me to southern India on several occasions to work on my yoga practice and become more deeply connected to myself.

Eastern philosophy is important in the lives and teachings of most of the masters, and many of them originate from the East. I really believe that there are masters from all cultures—some uncovered, some yet to be uncovered—but many spiritual traditions have been deeply influenced by the teachings of the East, and through some of the ideas of Eastern philosophy we can gain greater awareness of the concepts and energy the masters offer us.

Spiritual Similarities

Through my study of Eastern philosophy and yogic principles I've come to see that there are many corresponding and similar ideas in other traditions, which we are now coming into contact with. Here's a brief overview of some of the widely shared ideas that have led us to trust that these masters are real and of service to the Earth.

Shambhala and Shangri-La

In the Tibetan Buddhist tradition, Shambhala (also spelled Shambhalla) is a mystical land in what can only be described as another dimension. This sacred space, mentioned in the Kalachakra Tantra practice, as well as folklore and oral traditions, is said to be a golden land where many enlightened beings, bodhisattvas, and buddhas are gathered. Another common idea is that this group of golden beings will assemble at a future date to rid the world of all darkness. *(See also Chapter 4.)*

The Communion of Saints

In many branches of Christianity, including the Greek Orthodox, there's talk of a fellowship of both living and deceased souls who are dedicated to the wellbeing of the world. The idea is that they are all "knitted" together, as if by an unseen thread, through their communion to Christ. What fascinates me most is that there are prayer and contemplation services dedicated to these souls, in which people seek divine inspiration and leadership.

The Council of Light

In his 1795 book, *Cloud upon the Sanctuary*, the German mystic and philosopher Karl von Eckartshausen wrote about a "body of mystics who remained active after their physical death." If you ask me, this is likely to have influenced a lot of what we know today and also to have been the link between many other traditions. It certainly influenced many occult and Western Mystery Tradition leaders, such as the poet, mystic, and Hermetic Order of the Golden Dawn member A. E. Waite, the co-creator of the Rider-Waite Tarot, and the notorious black magician Aleister Crowley.

Today the Council of Light is a name that has resurfaced to describe the Ascended Masters.

The Secret Chiefs

The Hermetic Order of the Golden Dawn (Golden Dawn for short) was a secret society devoted to the study of magical, occult and metaphysical ideas. Many of its members, including Waite and Crowley, influenced the spiritual culture that we know today. Its initiatory system was very similar to that of Freemasonry, but a lot of its practices were more focused on the invocation of angels and on personal development through study of the Tarot, astrology, and the Kabbalah.

According to their teachings, the "Secret Chiefs" were "transcendent cosmic authorities" who could be called upon, invoked, and even met with on the "inner planes" of the spirit world.

Spiritual Teachers

To see that there's a thread running through these spiritual traditions that's similar to what we now refer to as the Ascended Master teachings excites me. It helps us see that many influences have come together to form what we know today.

Of course, in the four corners of the world, it's a common belief that the soul goes somewhere when we die. Also that there is someone or something watching over us. If we believe that ancestors and angels are there to guide us and protect us, it's not really that much of a stretch to believe that souls who have been through great learning experiences during their incarnations upon Earth are also offering their guidance from a spiritual dimension.

Many people have taught that this is happening. They have come from a variety of traditions and belief systems. It hasn't always been straightforward and all belief systems have had controversies, challenges, and egos getting in the way of the message from time to time. If I didn't point this out, I'd be doing you a disservice.

With that being said, let's look at some of the teachers in the Ascended Master world.

Helena Petrovna Blavatsky and Theosophy

All those who work with the Ascended Masters have undoubtedly been influenced by the work, findings, and experiences of one woman, Helena Petrovna Blavatsky, or HPB. She was born into an aristocratic Russian–German family in 1831 in what we now call Ukraine. It is said she was always quite the character, with things to say and questions to ask. Mostly self-educated, she was very well read and became deeply interested in spiritual matters, secret societies, and most likely Freemasonry, as her great-grandfather, Prince Pavel Vassilyevich Dolgorukov, was a Mason and had an extensive library featuring a lot of books about philosophy, spirituality, and occult matters.

After being married (supposedly to prove a point to her sister-in-law, who believed HPB was undesirable) for a mere three weeks, at just 17 years old, HPB set off on a spiritual quest. She later claimed that she traveled through Europe, the Americas, and India, and met living Masters of Ancient Wisdom, although some researchers argue that her story is somewhat fictitious.

By the 1870s she was definitely involved with the Spiritualist movement and in 1873 moved to New York City. It was there that she met Henry Steel Olcott, a military officer and lawyer who was a newspaper journalist at the time. An article of his in the New York *Sun* investigating Spiritualism attracted HPB's attention. They later met at a Spiritualist event and, as kindred spirits with a common interest in spiritual development, they, along with a few other people, founded the Theosophical Society (TS) in 1875.

This spiritual study and investigation group still exists today, describing itself as: "an unsectarian body of seekers after Truth, who endeavor to promote Brotherhood and strive to serve humanity." I've been to a branch in Glasgow a few times. The last meeting I attended there was a shamanic drumming circle. While the TS has a huge emphasis on Eastern religions and philosophy, it investigates the experience of spirituality whatever the context.

With Olcott's support, in 1877 HPB published her first book, *Isis Unveiled*, which brought together a variety of esoteric ideas and made it clear that her mission was to revive ancient wisdom. As a result, the Theosophical Society became widely known. One notable member, and friend to Blavatsky and Olcott, was the American inventor Thomas Edison.

The story goes that Henry Olcott experienced the full material manifestation of an Indian master by his bed in the middle of the night, guiding him to take the TS to India. He and Helena left a very comfortable life in New York for a three-month boat journey.

In February 1879, they arrived in Bombay (now Mumbai). It is said they kissed the ground upon arrival and were welcomed with open arms when the locals realized that they weren't Christian missionaries set on converting them from Indian religions.

In the July of the same year, they met Alfred Percy Sinnet, the editor of the *Pioneer*, an English-language newspaper still in circulation today. The meeting was arranged because Alfred was a keen Spiritualist and the TS had recently started its own monthly magazine, *The Theosophist*.

Upon hearing about "the Mahatmas," Sinnet was interested in having his own direct experience of them and convinced Blavatsky to facilitate this. Over the course of the next four years (1880–84), he received 1,400 pages of letters from the masters Koot Hoomi (KH) and Morya (M). Supposedly they arrived in various paranormal ways, such as manifesting in mid-air above someone's head or appearing in a wooden box in the middle of a wall during spiritual gatherings.

Unsurprisingly, there was a lot of speculation about where these "Mahatma Letters" or "Letters from the Masters" really came from. Some people thought the masters were real, some wondered if Blavatsky was writing the letters (maybe through automatic writing), or was receiving direct dictation from the masters, or if these particular masters were physical people or the fully realized spiritual forms of people she had met on her journeys through India, Tibet, and Egypt. The letters themselves were spiritual discourses sharing esoteric ideas in language that mixed Western terminology with Indo-Tibetan phraseology. At times they were hard to fathom, not unlike a lot of the channeled documents on the internet today.

In 1884, the Society for Psychical Research conducted a full investigation into the paranormal phenomena around Blavatsky, which concluded she was a fraud and the Mahatmas fictitious. It is, however, important to recognize that in 1986 these findings were reviewed and retracted. The Mahatma Letters are now in the British Library.

Although the Theosophical Society became firmly established in India, with a main HQ in Bombay, branches across the country, a lot of local members, and a few westerners who had strayed from the colonial world-view then in place, it seems it all became a bit much for HPB. From 1885 onward, as the TS experienced radical growth, with 121 lodges being established around the world, in deteriorating health, she accompanied Henry Olcott on a trip around Europe.

Arriving in London in 1887, she founded her own lodge, which drew in many of the London Theosophists. She also established the Theosophical Publishing Company and completed her next book, *The Secret Doctrine*, in which she outlined her ideas about the universe, the planets, humanity, the soul, and the afterlife. She was the first spiritual teacher to mention the Akashic records.

She finally handed over the reins of the Blavatsky Lodge in 1890 to a social and political activist named Annie Besant and established the European headquarters of the TS at Besant's house. She eventually died there, from influenza, on May 8th, 1891. To commemorate her death, a celebration is held every year on May 8th—known as White Lotus Day—by Theosophists the world over.

HPB's life certainly had some notable moments. She reportedly held a séance in the White House in Washington, DC, and inspired Mahatma Gandhi, who was an associate member of the London branch of the Theosophical Society when he was studying law, to read the *Bhagavad Gita*. The *Gita* became Gandhi's guide when he was returning India to independence. HPB was also hugely influential in that she was probably the first female spiritual seeker to immerse herself in Eastern traditions and so contributed to the craze of westerners going to places like Egypt and India to "find themselves." Basically, we can thank Blavatsky for *Eat, Pray, Love*.

I think it's important to share my own personal conclusions on these early masters, and of course HPB herself, and I highly encourage you to form your own. Of course her masters could have been real physical people, wandering yogis or wise men, or they could have been spirits she was encountering in transcendental meditation states. I believe that we all have the capacity to connect to the minds, hearts, and intelligence of beings on the other side of the veil. I believe we can call on those who have walked the Earth before us and ask them to guide us and help us to overcome challenges that are similar to the ones they faced.

With that being said, I'd heard about El Morya and Kuthumi before I researched HPB's life, and they had always felt real to me, so I think it is likely they were people she met on her journeys. The name Morya could have been used to protect the true identity of a living master, most likely Ranbir Singh, the Maharaja of Jammu and Kashmir, who interceded to stop the

British invading in 1845. Mysteriously, he died a year after the Mahatma Letters ceased. El Morya, as he's now known, is a master of spiritual protection who can guide us to create powerful boundaries in our life so that our energy is not invaded. (*See p.129.*)

Of course, some things aren't clear about the life, discoveries, and experiences of Helena Blavatsky, but what is clear is that she was powerful and influential. She has most likely influenced us all through uncovering Eastern mysteries and bringing them to the West. Sure, there was probably some showmanship associated with her practices, but what medium or spiritual teacher doesn't have that? Or an ego? It's also important to note that she didn't want to be a medium or convert people to believing in mediumship, but was more interested in creating a unified world that acknowledged we all have a spirit and consciousness. I believe her endeavors to create a sense of togetherness in philosophy and religion have borne fruit today. You can find Buddhist statues in Christian homes, for example, and more westerners than ever go East looking for answers. And of course the Ascended Masters' influence has continued…

Guy Warren Ballard and the "I AM" Activity

Guy Warren Ballard, an American mining engineer, was heavily influenced by his meetings with the Ascended Master Saint Germain, which began in the 1930s when they met at the foot of Mount Shasta, California. Under the pen name Godfré Ray King, he wrote the books *Unveiled Mysteries* and *The Magic Presence*, and with his wife, Edna, he created a movement known as the "I AM" Activity. This still exists today in the form of the Saint Germain Press.

The work conducted by the "I AM" Activity combines the power of the mind with affirmations and visualizations while welcoming in the presence of the masters. As this work originates from the 1930s United States, there is a strong Patriotic Christian undertone in the teachings. The Ballards claimed that they were the original and only accredited messengers of Saint Germain, but they considered Jesus highly important and also brought in other Ascended Masters such as Lady Nada and Archangel Michael.

Though a lot of the ideas and work of the "I AM" Activity and the Saint Germain Press can appear quite intense, clearly they have influenced modern spiritual practice. For example, the Sword of the Blue Flame, a sword that can free us from negativity, is quite similar to the sword I envision when I am calling on Archangel Michael to cut cords holding me to past fear. I also have to say that the artwork from the "I AM" Activity is beautiful.

The Prophets, the Church Universal and Triumphant, and the Summit Lighthouse

Mark L. Prophet and his wife, Elizabeth Clare Prophet, were highly controversial leaders of a religious sect who were strongly associated with some Ascended Master teachings. It's important to say, though, that they were clear examples of how ego and abuse of power can taint a spiritual mission.

Mark L. Prophet, a self-styled prophet, created the Church Universal and Triumphant, known as CUT for short and also called the Summit Lighthouse, in 1958. In the 1960s he met his soon-to-be-wife, Elizabeth, when she attended one of his meetings. Her mother was interested in Theosophy, the "I AM" Activity, and Christian Science. Elizabeth Clare Prophet became the leader of CUT in 1973.

CUT built up a following, and many people reported life-changing transformations. It shared teachings about the Ascended Masters, the Violet Flame, and spiritual retreats, which had clearly been influenced by the work of Helena Blavatsky and Guy Ballard, but in this case they were used in the creation of a new religious order with dogma, rules, and regulations. This did appeal, however, to baby boomers who wanted to make a positive difference in the world. Many went as far as to sell their businesses or cash in their life savings and donate them to CUT.

In 1989, Elizabeth Clare Prophet and the Summit Lighthouse found themselves receiving a great deal of unwanted publicity when it came to light that they had stockpiled weapons and begun to create bunkers at a US$17m dollar ranch in Montana, because Mark Prophet had predicted a nuclear war.

In a 2008 interview, Elizabeth Prophet's son said that his mother had admitted she had abused her power and had regrets about the unfolding of her career. She died in 2009 from Alzheimer's disease.

Alice Bailey

Alice Bailey was a British writer and medium. Born in 1880, she was linked with the Theosophical Society before going on to share her own teachings and methods of metaphysical practice in more than 20 books. She claimed they had been telepathically dictated to her by a master of wisdom known as "the Tibetan" or "DK," who was later revealed as Djwal Khul (*see p.123*).

Bailey believed that all traditional religious ideas led to the same place of love. She was the first to use and popularize the terms "Age of Aquarius" and "New Age." Her teachings are widely known and one of her prayers, "The

Great Invocation," written in 1937, is often shared at Spiritualist meetings and meditation gatherings and in response to tragic world events. Some of her work has recently been criticized as racist and anti-Semitic, including some of the language used in that prayer. It is true that a lot is outdated now, and the information on race is not an educated view. It is important, though, to note that Bailey's vision was a form of universal spirituality that transcended denominational identification and she believed that "every class of human beings is a group of brothers." ("Brothers" and "brotherhood" are terms often used in older new-thought texts that were influenced by the patriarchal systems of the time.)

Grace Cooke and the White Eagle Lodge

Grace Cooke was an early 20th-century British medium who received teachings from an Ascended Master called White Eagle and, with her husband, Ivan Cooke, founded the spiritual organization the White Eagle Lodge in 1936. The lodge is still active, with branches in America and Australia, and combines the teachings of White Eagle with Spiritualist ideas and a somewhat Christian approach. It teaches astrology and healing, and has been particularly influential in promoting "absent healing." If you have ever sent or received distant energy healing, then the work of Grace Cooke and White Eagle has contributed.

So here you have it—a brief history of the masters and the influence they have had on spiritual communities today.

CHAPTER 3

ASCENSION EXPLAINED

*"Ascend with the greatest awareness
from Earth to heaven. Unite with
the power of all things."*

THE EMERALD TABLET

The masters are acknowledged as "ascended" because they have heightened perception and awareness and have returned to the spiritual realm. In their last lifetime they experienced an initiatory chain of life events and circumstances that led them to a deeper understanding of life and love. In my interpretation, these "initiations" were genuinely challenging circumstances that they had no option but to overcome. A great example would be El Morya protecting his country from the British invaders. This gave him a deepened awareness of what it takes to protect people and keep them safe. So, from an ascended space, his energy is dedicated to helping create boundaries, remove negative forces from our life, and protect our energy.

What Is Ascension?

A Christian Tradition

The word "ascension" has been taken from the biblical narrative of Christ's ascent to heaven. In short, the story goes that 40 days after his resurrection, Jesus led 11 followers to the village of Bethany, on the Mount of Olives, where he gave guidance and prophesied that his name would be known the world over. Then he began to rise upward until he disappeared into the clouds. Afterwards, two men (most likely angels) appeared in the crowd dressed completely in white, saying that Jesus had returned to God. They added that he would return to Earth, though they didn't specify how or when.

Even if this ascension story isn't literally true, it's a powerful allegory illustrating that we have the capacity to rise up and return beyond death. I believe that when the angels said that Jesus would return, they meant spiritually—that he would be able to commune with his followers from beyond the veil. In fact he would remain with them through their heart connection.

There's a similar story relating to Mary, the mother of Christ. In her case, at the end of her life, when her physical body was ready to die, her soul "assumed" its rightful position in heaven. This is known as the Assumption.

Ascension has become a great desire for many walking the spiritual path today, although to be quite frank, everyone has different ideas on how it will unfold. But even if those who are walking the ascension pathway aren't fully aware of the Christian teachings around ascension, they'll still be influenced by them. Influence can exist without dogma—that's my opinion, anyway. So you'll find some who believe that one day, if they prepare themselves properly, their physical body will become one of light and they'll float into the clouds or "move into the fifth dimension," while others, more influenced by the story of Mary, believe that when it comes to their physical body's passing, their soul will ascend into the fifth dimension or the spiritual realms and they'll continue their journey to mastery from that space.

In my view, ascension isn't about leaving the body, but fully arriving in the body and meeting our spirit there. It's about holding our body with love, guiding our life from our heart, and recognizing that within us there is a presence—an eternal presence of light. It's knowing that when our body dies, that presence, that spark, will live on, and what it's learnt, through the experiences we've had, will be carried back to the heart of the universe.

Samadhi

Samadhi is a deep meditative state of consciousness that is part of many Eastern traditions such as Hinduism, Jainism, Buddhism, and Sikhism. In Sanskrit, the word means "to collect together" or "to gather." It represents the whole self. But it goes beyond the self. Ultimately, *samadhi* is a state of absolute bliss in which we are aligned to the whole. Instead of acting from ego or even intellect, we are experiencing the world from a heightened consciousness state of love. In yogic teaching, the aim is to reach this state of ultimate bliss and connectedness through the practice of yoga and meditation. For me, it feels like what we're trying to achieve through the process of ascension.

It's also a state that many of us can reach through our spiritual practice. We'll have snippets of this bliss in our life, moments when we'll know we are part of something greater and will feel united with the Source of creation. Traditional yogic art and even some Buddha statues show the master with his eyes nearly closed, experiencing *samadhi*. When I see a friend having a moment of bliss, I call it *"samadhi* eyes." To see someone light up from the inside like this is a God experience moment!

Maha is Sanskrit for "great," and there's also a process called *maha-samadhi*, which occurs at the end of a yogi's life. Many of the great Indian stories relate instances of this and it is mentioned in *Autobiography of a Yogi* by Paramahansa Yogananda. What happens is the yoga master moves into a deep meditative state, and instead of coming out of it at the end of the meditation, they cross over. I love the idea that they move into such a deep state of peace that they are eventually able to be consumed by light once more.

When we hear these stories, we may get concerned about moving into deep meditation, but those who experience *maha-samadhi* are experienced practitioners and enlightened beings who have completed all of their duties here on Earth and have chosen to go home to the light.

Ultimately, ascension isn't about leaving or transforming the physical body, but about creating and harnessing a connection with consciousness. It's about waking up, raising our vibration, and living a heart-based life. Truth be told, the process is unfolding for all of us who walk the spiritual path. It begins when we have what is known as an "awakening"—when we realize that there's something more to life than what to have for dinner, that our life hasn't happened by mistake, and that ultimately that we have a purpose, we're part of a bigger picture.

A Goal

Though the idea of ascension has been packaged differently around the world and in different traditions, it's similar to enlightenment—the Western term for the Buddhist concept of "awakening." In all spiritual paths there is something of a "goal," or, if you don't like that word, an intention. When we undertake something, whether it be learning a sport or even going on a diet, we want something to happen as a result of that process. Spiritual practice is the same. Our "want" or "intention" in undertaking it need not be a selfish one; it can genuinely come from the heart and be in the best interests of all. We may get into meditation or spirituality because we want to become a more positive person, for example, or to be a better person for our family to have around. I believe the process of ascension is all about serving and contributing to the experience of others.

I also feel that if we live out our life and fulfill our mission on Earth, when it comes to the death of our physical body, instead of being given an opportunity to reincarnate, we have the opportunity to continue serving the Earth as a spiritual guide or master. That's what the masters were able to do and is what we're striving to do through the process of ascension. Ascension is about aligning our life to the light and having the intention that all we do will have a loving effect on the world. It might not even unfold in this lifetime—it could be many in the making—but what an intention to have!

The Process of Ascension

For me, the process of ascension is about raising our vibration, overcoming all forms of karma, fully embodying the energy of forgiveness, and living a heart-centered life.

Raising Our Vibration

The ascension process is ultimately about becoming a lighthouse and shining as brightly as possible. To do this, we need to do the deep inner work to fully know ourselves and raise our vibration. Even if ascension isn't a conscious goal, the process unfolds naturally for anyone who is deeply driven to become the best version of themselves; anyone who selflessly aligns to living purposefully is walking the ascension pathway. They are embodying the qualities of an earth angel—someone who intentionally raises their vibrational frequency to bring waves of love, goodness, and kindness to the planet.

Raising our vibration means aligning every action, non-action, choice, and experience with the light. It's about being aware of our influence on others, contributing positively to the world, and leaving the Earth better than we found it.

There's no way to fast-forward the ascension process, though. We cannot become "too high vibe" for challenging stuff. Ascension work is about facing darkness head on, dealing with the shadow-self and even facing the aspects of ourselves that we'd prefer to avoid. All of this can be achieved by doing one thing: aligning to purpose.

Overcoming Karmic Lessons

Karma is a chain of action and events. Often it is misunderstood or misinterpreted as "what goes around comes around," but it's more than that. It's the law of cause and effect, a spiritual force that helps unfold what is yet to come. What I've learnt about karma from the Indo-Tibetan traditions is that it's less about punishment and more about acting with purpose, compassion, and kindness. The idea is that through living a life of loving-kindness and generosity, we will have fewer challenges and limitations in the lifetimes that are yet to come.

Karma unfolds differently for everyone, but I believe overcoming it is about taking every challenging moment head on or, when we have the opportunity and the mental and emotional resources, undoing any damage that has been created for us or by us.

When we speak about undoing karma, we're referring to the challenges that we have yet to face head on. These challenges can be lessons from a previous lifetime that are being continued in this lifetime or issues from a past experience that have been buried and not resolved. Usually, we're aware of a lesson we need to learn or issue we need to resolve in our current lifetime—it could be something we're avoiding dealing with right now. Whenever we face challenges that we'd prefer to avoid and become clearer about what we need to do in order to fulfill our purpose, we are undoing karmic lessons. This is what the masters consider initiatory experiences.

Embodying Forgiveness and Living a Heart-Centered Life

I've learnt that forgiveness is many things. It isn't about just "letting something go" or "letting someone get away with their bad decisions" or spiritually bypassing bad life choices in our own past, it's about choosing to rise beyond all of these situations, healing the wounds we may have inflicted or suffered, and consciously making changes to live from the highest state possible in the future. It's ultimately a correction to our vision. It's about choosing to see the world through the eyes of love. This includes ourselves. Forgiveness is the moment when we reclaim our innocence, the moment we realize that we lacked judgment or awareness in a past situation. Forgiveness is trusting that we can use what we know now to make better, more informed choices. It's about no longer allowing someone else's poor judgment or bad decisions to stand in the way of our growth, freedom, and joy. Forgiveness is about embodying peace. It's about experiencing vulnerability in order to reach fearlessness. It's the moment we are humane. Through forgiveness we can authentically live a heart-centered life.

Living a heart-centered life is basically what it says on the tin: living from the heart. For me, it's about being conscious of our decisions, actions, and non-actions. It's about really checking in to make sure that not only are we serving others through our life choices, but also that we are being served and sustained during that process. It's about self-mastery.

Self-Mastery

Self-mastery is becoming fully aware of who we are. It's knowing our emotions and becoming one with them, rather than avoiding or suppressing them. With self-mastery, instead of being reactive, we are aware of our emotions as they rise up and we acknowledge that they are powerful messengers from within. Just like the master yogi/yogini experiencing *samadhi*, instead of reacting from the selfish self, we have a composed, informed, and loving approach to all that we are doing. We step into a space of equanimity, of pure vulnerability and bravery. Self-mastery is ultimately awakening the inner buddha and allowing that great teacher to rise up and out.

Heaven on Earth

Living a heart-centered life is also about experiencing heaven on Earth, *samadhi*, pure bliss, and the interconnectedness of all things. Instead of wanting to ascend beyond the body, we ascend within it. Many think that ascension is about rising beyond the body, and I think ultimately it is, but the time between birth and physical death must include embodiment. Embodiment is about fully arriving in our body and loving the skin we're in. It's about recognizing that we have a soul, but that soul is housed within our body. Our body is a vehicle, and that vehicle needs us to respect it, connect with it, and care for it. I have learnt through the teachings of my friend the scholar Meggan Watterson that in Greek this vehicle is known as *anthropos*—fully human, fully divine.

Living in a way that is fully human and fully divine and experiencing the interconnectedness of all things is an indescribable state that all of us crave deeply. The human craves connection by default; the soul longs for the human to remember the connection to Oneness.

Then, when the time of transition comes and we leave this vehicle behind, ascension is about knowing we have lived our best life, cleared all our unfinished business, embodied our light, and are now moving to our rightful place within the cosmos.

Ascended Masters have completed this process. So, not only can they guide us through our life experiences, they can become role-models for us. Seeing what they have been able to achieve encourages us to step onto the path of light and live fully.

I honestly believe that many people doing great work on Earth have the potential to become a master, or at least, when they transition, become a spiritual guide. Truth be told, not all of the masters listed in this book knew they would reach that spiritual level, and I don't think it was their goal either. They were just living heart-centered lives. I think we should do the same. They can show us how, if we connect with them.

CHAPTER 4

THE HIGH COUNCIL AND ETHERIC RETREATS

"As we approach the golden age, the veils shall
be removed and the people of the earth shall
become aware of the people of the universe."

EDGAR CAYCE

The idea of a congregation of enlightened beings gathering together in a magical land, spiritual world, or different dimension has been explored in spiritual traditions the world over. This congregation of enlightened ones, cosmic light beings, Ascended Masters, and angels is known by many names, including the Secret Chiefs, the Great White Brotherhood (though it does include females), and the Council of Light. Many of the masters who are part of it are mentioned in this book and many others are beyond our vibrational reach. They have been the way-showers for hundreds, even thousands, of years.

This high council, as I will call it, keeps the Akashic records, the spiritual "book" that records every happening the world over—every up, every down, every experience of every incarnation ever. After our return to spirit, we use these records to review our life, to take an inventory of our achievements, and to understand our karma. It is then that we are offered the opportunity to reincarnate and continue learning or step into other spiritual roles, such as becoming a spirit guide and, in some cases, a master.

I'm not sure about you, but I have soul memories, flickering memories from before I was in this body, from when I was back in the spiritual realms. I remember sitting at a giant table in a room filled with light with other beings and Divine Masters. I felt that I was in the presence of greatness and family all at the same time. I remember talking about life contracts and soul lessons, and hoping that in this lifetime I would remember my cosmic origins. I also remember knowing that these masters would become part of my spiritual evolution and that I would be able to contact them from the Earth realm.

I know I'm not the only soul who's sat at that table. Many of us who feel called to develop spiritually have visited that council chamber many times, in preparation for many lifetimes. It doesn't feel as though that space exists in linear time, but beyond it. Writing about it, it's almost as though I'm back there now, in a higher dimension or other universe.

I believe that we all have the capacity to remember aspects of these meetings with the high council of spiritual elders and the review of our soul's growth. I believe we have the capacity to tap into what we have learnt over our many incarnations. In fact I believe that you aren't reading this book and feeling intuitively called to connect with the masters just because you're curious or because you want to learn, but because you're unlocking memories on a spiritual level.

The idea of being able to remember beyond this lifetime isn't new. Neither is the idea of choosing to reincarnate. It is said that His Holiness the Dalai

Lama can choose whether to reincarnate or not, as can other lamas. Right now, in the year 2020, we have the pleasure of being on the same planet as Tenzin Gyatso, the 14th Dalai Lama. That means he's the 14th incarnation of the same soul. At the end of each life, he will give an indication of where in the world he will reincarnate, and then a search party will go and look for that incarnation. When this is found, usually in the form of a very young boy, a number of tests will be conducted to see if he really is the reincarnated Dalai Lama. These include identifying personal items, such as prayer beads, from the previous incarnation. So, the Dalai Lama assumes his position based on past-life information being remembered in his present life. I find that very cool.

Do you have memories of a past life? Have you ever been somewhere that felt familiar, but you didn't know why? Do you resonate with a certain saint, master, or teacher from the past? Maybe it's because you were with them in a previous life. Or on the other side. Do you ever feel that you've been before the high council? What did they say?!

Etheric Retreats

The "space" in which the high council sits is an etheric retreat. These retreats are otherworldly places that we can visit in the dream state, in meditation, and between lifetimes. They are energetic portals to deep spiritual learning. Even if we don't remember what happens when we go there, I know that we receive information that we can access when we need it.

I remember discovering etheric retreats. It was when I was sitting in a circle with other developing mediums. Coming together on a regular basis to meditate was so powerful. I owe a lot of my spiritual growth to that time. Normally, we'd be led on a guided meditation somewhere like a beach or a cave where we'd meet loved ones and sometimes our spiritual guides. I loved these meditations and as the years went on, they became longer and we'd go deeper and deeper. Then one night, when I must have been about 16, my teacher decided that we were all to go on our own journey.

I remember that particular night because when she sent us off on our own it felt as though a huge shift had occurred. I remember the music so clearly. It was Native American chanting—piercing, painful, and powerful at the same time. The thumping drum and the constant chant were hypnotic. I remember finding myself continually swallowing and feeling as if I was falling forward in my body—you know that feeling you get when you're falling asleep on a flight or in the back of the car? That feeling.

I was going deeper and deeper, when all of a sudden I found myself in a gigantic building. The floor was black and white tiles—think masonic temple meets Chanel fashion show. When I moved my feet, I heard an echo, because the walls were so far apart and the rafters so high. I remember seeing a huge staircase that unfolded to the left and right and being met by a being, but I can't remember their face or what happened after that. I just know that something great happened.

When I came back to myself, about 40 minutes had passed, but it felt as if it had been five. Later, we were all asked to share our experiences. When it was my turn, before I could even speak, someone said, "Well, we know Kyle's is going to be a good one… Did anyone else see his soul leave his body?" and then someone else said, "I thought it was just me, but in my meditation, I saw Kyle walk past as if he was going to the next room. I just assumed he was going to the bathroom or something."

My teacher, who was an extremely capable medium, explained that I had indeed left the room. "Kyle astral-projected, and now he can tell us where he went!"

"I did?" I said. "I thought I was just falling asleep because I kept falling forward."

"You didn't fall forward, Kyle. You sat upright the whole time. But I saw your spirit leave your physical body and go through some sort of portal."

I was surprised in one way, but in another I wasn't. I began to share my experience with the circle.

"You went to the Great Halls of Learning, or what some call the Halls of Learning," my teacher told me. "Some of the best mediums I know have reported being taken to that spiritual retreat. It's a place where great masters transfer information into your being that will help your spiritual evolution."

So that was the night I was reintroduced to the etheric retreats of the masters.

We don't need to meditate to access these places. I know for a fact that many of us have dreams in which we go to them. I couldn't even count the number of dreams I've had where I've been walking on sacred lands, running with wild animals, and living in harmony with nature. I've had dreams in which I've visited lamas in the Himalayas and sacred temples at the heart of pyramids. I know these dreams are a mixture of soul memories and spaces that I've projected myself into via the astral realms.

If all of this seems familiar, trust that it is. You are going through a process similar to the one I went through, uncovering your spiritual truth and remembering the sacred information that is stored within your being. This is a very special time.

There are a lot of ideas out there on spiritual and ethereal retreats, and I think it's important to remember that spiritual experiences are often very personal and it's okay for contrasting information to exist. All of us are processing our experiences through the understanding of the human shell that we are in at this time.

Have you ever been to a retreat? Have you ever been taken somewhere in a dream or meditation? Do you remember visiting a temple, a giant hall, or a magical kingdom?

Here are a few experiences that are common when you're visiting a spiritual retreat in dreams or meditation:

- You feel or dream that you are leaving your body and visiting a faraway land.
- You don't know where you are, but it feels familiar.
- You see bright colors and fine details.
- You feel you aren't alone.
- You come into contact with spiritual masters, elders, or other beings of light.
- When you wake up, you know that you've been traveling in your sleep.

I believe the purpose of visiting etheric retreats is to have a direct experience of the energy we connect with in prayer. When we go to these sacred spaces, we have the most incredible experiences and feel connected to something greater than ourselves.

We also receive energetic upgrades, transmissions, and activations. Light-coded information is taken directly from the Source of teaching into our energy field and is then revealed in the perfect time–space sequence.

It's similar to being attuned to an energy healing system such as Reiki: you receive a direct transmission of energy codes, information, and light to support you as your path unfolds.

Here's a list of some etheric retreats, but know there are many more throughout the divine matrix (*see Chapter 5*). You might come across others during your own meditation and dreaming practices.

The Great Halls of Learning

These halls are the location of a sacred mystery school where we can go to develop our spiritual connection. It is particularly valuable for those who are working with mediumship or developing their ability to channel energies.

The Violet Flame

The Violet Flame is an etheric retreat dedicated to transmutation and transformation. This gigantic violet- and sometimes gold-colored flame has the ability to help us perform spiritual alchemy. By placing our fears or concerns into it, we step into a space of surrender and allow the energies of darkness and fear to be burnt away and reborn as light, like a phoenix rising from the ashes.

See also Lady Portia (p.215) and Saint Germain (p.224).

The Halls of Amenti

The Halls of Amenti are where the energies of the *Emerald Tablet* (*see p.251*) are stored. Governed by Thoth, they are said to be a sacred learning space that was energetically transported from Atlantis to an etheric space above or within the Great Pyramid of Giza. We don't have to go to Egypt physically to experience it, as it is an energetic space. We can go there to be initiated into the ways of divine magic so that we can harness and work with the energies of heaven and Earth. Many have reported seeing the Halls of Amenti as a room filled with pillars, a temple-like space with a huge altar and bright emerald green colors around everything.

See also Thoth (p.248).

Shambhala

Shambhala, also known as Shambhalla or Shangri-La, is a hidden city of light said to be found somewhere in the Himalayas near Tibet. It is strongly associated with Eastern traditions, including Buddhism. According to Theosophical teachings, this sacred etheric retreat is where we can come into contact with some of the greatest spiritual adepts, enlightened teachers, and Divine Masters who have ever walked the Earth. In Buddhism and Hinduism, Shambhala is said to be the home space for Shiva and for buddhas (enlightened beings), and in the Bon tradition every year thousands make a pilgrimage to Mount Kailash, the supposed location of the hidden city, which is said to bring good fortune.

The Hidden Temples of the Himalayas

In his book *Autobiography of a Yogi*, Paramahansa Yogananda writes about his experience of being transported to a hidden temple in the Himalayas and encountering Mahavatar Babaji (*see p.105*). In many yogic traditions it is believed that some of the greatest spiritual adepts, wandering men, and yogis entered such a deepened awakened state that they were able to transcend life and death and reach these hidden temples, where all the great teachings of yogic traditions are stored.

Lemuria and Lemurian Healing Temples

Lemuria is said to have been an ancient civilization in the Pacific Ocean. It is believed that the inhabitants of this sacred land lived in complete harmony with nature and, similar to the movie *Avatar*, had a connection with every living being and transcended physical existence.

Although the physical Lemuria is long gone, there are still spiritual impressions of it and its healing waters, and many spiritual practitioners have been transported there to receive spiritual upgrades and divine healing. If you feel particularly connected to Lemuria, it may be that you had a past life there or that a soul who was a healer or wise person there is now one of your spirit guides.

Physical Locations

There's a lot of information out there about certain physical locations having spiritual retreats either "within" or "over" them on a multi-dimensional level. From my own experience, I don't think that from our human viewpoint we can fully comprehend all the spiritual dimensions that actually exist. What I do know for sure is that there are many retreats and ethereal spaces that we can visit, and if you feel that you've been to some sort of sacred land, either in a dream or meditation or past life, I believe you!

A lot of spiritual authors also say that some physical locations, like Mount Shasta, are the physical retreats of the masters. There are a lot of sacred places on the Earth and I feel that the accumulation of energies at these spiritual "hotspots" can make it possible for us to venture into the spiritual realms from them. I know when I was at the Arulmigu Arunachaleswarar Temple in Tiruvannamalai, India, I saw angels like I'd never seen angels before.

When I was in Glastonbury, in the southwest of England, I experienced the presence of the Black Madonna in an extremely powerful way. So I understand why a lot of these incredibly spiritual places, especially in the last few hundred years, have been linked to Ascended Masters.

With that being said, I feel that giving an Ascended Master a location in a mundane sense is extremely limiting. From what I've learnt, we can connect to the Masters and Ancient Wisdom wherever we are and whenever we like. I also think we have to go beyond the Earth and realize that the masters' energies reside in spaces way beyond our comprehension.

The only two exceptions I make when it comes to the masters being at certain locations are for the hidden temples of the Himalayas and the hidden city of Shambhala. These places have been part of Eastern belief systems for hundreds and possibly thousands of years. But, although they are considered to be physical locations, I believe they are in fact spiritual retreats that cannot be visited in the body but only through spiritual experiences.

Remember, you can connect to the masters anywhere.

PART II

MAKING THE
CONNECTION

I call upon the Divine Masters, ancient
wisdom-keepers, the Council of Light.

Great gathering of souls, thank you for helping me
have a visceral understanding of ascension.

I am willing to be shown, taught, and guided.

Thank you for downloading into my frequency information
that will support my personal spiritual quest and endeavors.

With gentleness, show me, in my dreams, meditations,
and moments of contemplation, information
that will help me embody this knowing.

Thank you for directing me to insightful,
truthful, and enlightening information.

Thank you for guiding me to experience a moment of samadhi.

I am open to experiencing connectedness and bliss.

I am willing.

And so it is.

CHAPTER 5

THE DIVINE MATRIX

"Whatever affects one directly, affects all indirectly. I
can never be what I ought to be until you are what you
ought to be. This is the interrelated structure of reality."

MARTIN LUTHER KING JR.

The entire universe is connected. Everything that was, is, and ever will
be is connected through an invisible bond of energy, uniting every
living being from the past, present, and even future.

This information is not new. We've heard it from the likes of Jesus, Buddha,
and even Bob Marley. Today, scientists are beginning to provide evidence to
help us understand this bond.

Albert Einstein was an incredible man whose work not only supported the
evolution of science, but also understanding of the human spirit. In one of
his most famous quotes, which I often refer to in my lectures, workshops,
and talks, he stated: "Energy cannot be destroyed, it can only be changed
from one form to another."

To me, that feels quite simple and approachable. Energy is indestructible, but it can change form. For me, the soul is energy. This energy resides within our human shell and will do so until that human shell is ready to take its next form. It reminds me of the journey a caterpillar takes to become a butterfly, how it goes through a radical transformation to become an even more beautiful version of itself.

I've always been fascinated by the concept of Oneness. At the beginning of every one of my talks and workshops, I like to remind the participants that we've all come from the same Source of creation and we will all return to that same Source. No one is more sacred or special than anyone else. We are all equal.

We're also connected. We may not fully comprehend how we're connected, but we know it's true. I like to call our connection the "divine matrix," and I know it's also been referred to as "the field" and "the bond." It's the universal mind, the power, the light, the quantum field, and also what we're referring to when we use the singular term "spirit." It's the place we're all going to "one day," but it's also the place we're in right now.

The best way for me to describe it is like a lattice. We're all points on this grid and connected by it. I am connected to you and you are connected to me. We're both connected to all of our ancestors and loved ones. We're even connected to all the different aspects of ourselves, past, present, and future, as well as all the great minds who ever were, are, and will be. You are connected to angels and masters and enlightened beings right now. And through this invisible bond of energy, we all have the capacity to access the divine intelligence that's pulsing through the matrix.

The reason we're not always aware of this connection, or intelligence, is because it's operating on a different vibration from what we know in the third-dimensional world. In order to align with it, we have to raise our own vibration. We need to set an intention to move from the third-dimensional state into a higher-dimensional state. This can be achieved through deep breathing and meditation.

I remember meditating one day and asking to be shown "the true meaning of it all." I've always had big questions about how the universe was created and how it all works. That day I was trying to figure out how angels fitted into the bigger picture. Since I'd spent the majority of my life working with them, it seemed a natural enough question.

When I asked to be shown "the true meaning of it all," I remember seeing a huge golden flower of life shape and being instantly transported to what I can only describe as the heart of the universe. It was like looking into one of those plasma globes you see in science centers, or into a lava lamp, like the ones that almost everyone in my class in high school received for Christmas in the early 2000s. The main source of energy was in the center, and from that source, extensions of energy were carrying the light outward. Each strand was individual, but they were all very much part of one whole.

Angels and masters, I realized, were similar—connected to one Source, but expressing themselves individually. This vision also helped me to understand that the "hierarchy" of the Divine isn't so much vertical as circular—we are all gathering and expressing energy from the heart of the universe. We all have our own part to play, but we are all made up of that one energy. Nothing is separate. No one is separate. We're *all* expressions of that central ball of energy, like the waves of energy individually dancing in a plasma globe.

That same vision led me to recognize that whenever we call on angels, guides, or masters, we're calling on the heart of creation. Whenever we connect with the mind of a Divine Master, we're connecting directly with the divine mind of creation.

That vision helped me understand so much, but why exactly had I been shown the huge golden flower of life?

Shapes of Connection

The Flower of Life

Glyphs and images of the flower of life have been found the world over, including on pillars in Egypt that date back over 5,000 years, and it isn't connected to any particular religious or spiritual pathways. Which is appropriate, because it represents the connectedness of all things.

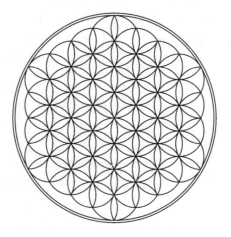

The flower of life

I had been seeing the flower of life in spiritual circles for a long time, and quite honestly, seeing it in the vision that day, I just thought, *Ah, what a lovely representation of the connection of all things*, not realizing that the flower of life really is a powerful illustration of the connectedness of the universe. I like sacred geometry, I think it's beautiful, but it wasn't until I was doing the research for this book that I started to recognize that the flower of life literally is a two-dimensional image of the divine matrix. It is therefore also a powerful image that we can focus on and meditate with in order to activate our divine potential and draw the intelligence of the masters to us.

The flower of life is basically 19 perfectly overlapping circles creating 36 arches, but when you begin to look more deeply into it, you find other images and information are revealed. Within the flower of life you can find geometry, structures, even the Fibonacci sequence. Here are just some of the forms you'll find.

DNA

DNA is the carrier of genetic information and is found in nearly all living organisms, including you and me. To think that we can find an image of our DNA within the flower of life is fascinating and a reminder that our human self is aligned with the greater picture and the Divine.

A strand of DNA

I am also fascinated by the fact that the DNA strand found in the flower of life is extremely similar to the orbits of Sirius A and B. Sirius is a binary star system whose two stars, A and B, orbit each other over the course of 50 years. They both have strong connections to star beings (*see p.245*).

The Egg of Life

This image is a gathering of circles that is identical to the cellular embryonic structure when it's in its third division. You may remember from biology class that when a cell develops, it multiplies. We all started back there, as little eggs, before growing into what we know today.

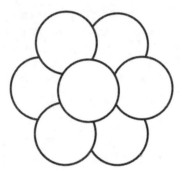

The egg of life

The Fruit of Life

The fruit of life is a gathering of 13 circles that mimics the structure of atoms and molecules.

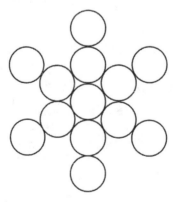

The fruit of life

Metatron's Cube

When you join the circles of the fruit of life, you get Metatron's cube, which contains all the Platonic solids relating to the five elements from ancient alchemy:

- Hexahedron: Earth
- Octahedron: Air
- Tetrahedron: Fire
- Icosahedron: Water
- Dodecahedron: Ether

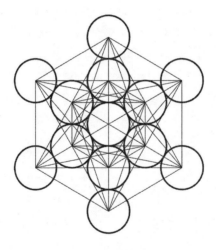

Metatron's cube

Aligning to the Matrix

You might be wondering what the divine matrix has to do with the Divine Masters. If you are, first of all, I respect and honor your inquiry. It's important to ask questions and to feel things out.

The reason the divine matrix is important is simple: connectedness. You are part of the divine matrix so beautifully depicted in the flower of life, and so are the masters. Therefore their wisdom and guidance are available to you at all times. *How cool is that?*

Connecting to the divine matrix is simple, because you already are. You are living, breathing, and experiencing it right now. Place your hands on your heart. It's a walkie-talkie of sorts, allowing you to connect consciously to the matrix. To the masters.

Using the Flower

The flower of life is another powerful tool for connecting consciously to the divine matrix. It allows us to realize our connection to the world and, even more importantly, our significance in it. It draws together all aspects of creation. It represents our DNA, the cells that multiplied to create us, the elements that stream through our being, the atoms and molecules that create our being and allow us to be, and the fact that we are aligned with everything that is.

When writing this book, I really wanted to learn more about sacred geometry and connect with the divine matrix through the flower of life. Connect consciously, I mean, because the more aware I become of sacred geometry, the more I realize I've unconsciously been using it in my home for several years. In 2017, at the Angel Congress in Salzburg, Austria, there was a stall in the spiritual marketplace that was selling lots of different items illustrating sacred geometry. I remember not having a lot of time in the marketplace but really wanting to buy something from this company. I said to my promoter, "Give me five minutes," and I just grabbed a bunch of stuff and paid up. I remember it coming to more than I thought and the seller handing me a brown paper bag full of the things I'd purchased. How easy it is to get carried away! I'd bought three cut-outs of sacred geometric shapes. One of them was a fiber-glass seed of life, another was a metal crop circle of an angel about 8 × 8 inches in size, and the last was a gold-plated flower of life. Yes, gold-plated. I am honestly too fancy for my own good.

I didn't take them out of the bag until I was home. Then I very unconsciously placed the seed of life on my altar, which is downstairs by the front window, I hung the angel crop circle up directly across from my bed, as if it was "looking over me," and I placed the gold-plated flower of life on my nightstand. They've all stayed there ever since. So when I started to think about the divine matrix being represented by the flower of life, I started to meditate with the gold one, and I left crystals on it at bedtime. Whenever I needed a power-up, I'd place those crystals on my chakra points and do a "power-nap" meditation for about 15 minutes. I had the feeling that in order to really understand the sacredness of sacred geometry, I had to let the frequency of it "in."

Then one night it dawned on me: in order to *really* get inside the flower of life, I needed to draw it. So I grabbed my lil' gold-plated one, a sketchbook, and a pen, and I began to trace around the first circle, then the second, third, and fourth. Somehow drawing the structure felt natural. I was doing it without really thinking about it. It seems drawing sacred geometry is something you don't just learn from doing, but something you can tap into through meditation. Soon I was drawing flowers of life in notebooks, on notebooks, on sketch paper, and on any available blank space. Why not try it for yourself?

DRAWING THE FLOWER OF LIFE

I recommend using a circular protractor or a compass to draw your flower. I find that I'm not as careful when using a compass, but if it's something you feel comfortable using, then use one. You can also use a coin or anything else that's circular and flat, though it becomes more complicated if you can't see through what you're using to align the central axis points.

I have a whole sketchbook dedicated to sacred geometry, but you can literally draw on anything from notebooks to the back of envelopes. I've seen the flower and seed of life chalked on sidewalks. They always make me smile.

Once you have everything ready:

✧ Take your circular protractor or compass and draw a circle in the center of the paper.

✧ Now take the central axis point of your protractor to the edge of the first circle and draw a second circle. You will now have a *vesica piscis* that looks like this:

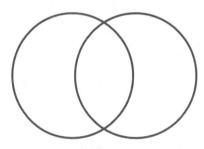

The vesica piscis

✧ Now go to the opposite edge of the central circle, align the end of your protractor with the edge of the second circle and the central axis with the line of the first and draw your next circle.

✧ Do the same diagonally and you'll have five circles.

✧ Now in the four corners you'll have *vesica* egg-style shapes. Take the central axis of the protractor again and align it with the edge touching the center of the "flower" and the central axis aligning with the line within each of the *vesica* shapes. You will now have nine overlapping circles in perfect formation. This is the seed of life. In it, you can also find the egg of life. You are aligning with the energies of human creation.

✧ This is where it gets super fun and exciting. Now, where every two circles overlap, align the center of your protractor (or point of your compass) and draw a circle. When you've done so, continue extending outward and you will have the flower of life.

✧ The goal is to have a flower five circles long and five circles wide, which will allow you to see the fruit of life and Metatron's cube.

I suggest you experiment with different versions of the geometry and even take a ruler and join up lines to make structures. But before you do, I recommend trying the following exercise to connect consciously with the matrix.

Connecting with the Divine Matrix

Once you've completed a flower of life, hold it in your hands, gaze at the central point, and breathe deeply.

As you gaze at the center, realize that it is emblematic of your connection to everything that is.

Affirm:

> *I am one with all that is, infinitely connected to life.*
>
> *I am one with all that is, filled with love and light.*
>
> *I am one with all that is. Divine intelligence is available to me now.*
>
> *I am one with all that is, aligned with the divine matrix.*

Be still. Feel connected.

The Seven Spiritual Rays

The seven spiritual rays appear in many schools of thought the world over. The number seven has been deemed sacred for several reasons, including the fact that there are seven days in the week, seven continents, seven oceans, and even seven vertebrae in the neck and seven layers of skin on the body.

The seven spiritual rays are considered to be extensions of divine energy that allow us to draw down and embody energetic support in a number of areas in our life. Each ray is associated with an archangel and Ascended Master, who are essentially the energetic guardians of these divine sources of energy.

Just as with most aspects of modern-day spirituality, there are a lot of contrasting ideas out there with regard to the spiritual rays. I spent a good while puzzling over it all before I realized that I had to ask my angelic guides and the Divine Masters to impart the information I needed. In reply, I received the strong feeling that I already knew and had shared the information, I'd just never really put it together.

Thinking about it, I realized I'd always paired certain archangels up with colors, and my understanding of their gifts and healing purpose had been based on my interpretations of the colors I'd seen when connecting with them. I'd written extensively about archangels in my book *Angel Prayers*, and the approach I'd taken then was similar to the approach I'd been taking when putting together information about the Divine Masters for this book. So, it was true—I just had to put the information together and continue what I was doing.

To understand the spiritual rays, think of a diamond. When it is kissed by light, it will light up inside and radiate light, which will be reflected by other surfaces. These reflections will be in rainbow colors, and depending on where they are, some colors will be clearer and more prevalent than others. Source is that diamond. It is a light-bearer and a light-sharer. Each shade of light that it radiates has different qualities and gifts. When we connect with particular masters, we may see or feel drawn to a particular color. This is a message and also a download of the energetic frequencies that this master is bringing us.

The seven spiritual rays are often put in a certain order, as if to indicate some sort of hierarchy of spiritual awareness. I've been informed by my guides that this is simply not the case and that the spiritual rays aren't coming from the heart of Source in a linear fashion but more of a circular one. I was shown an image of the spiritual realms as a sphere of infinite light radiating in seven directions. Each direction is a spiritual ray that can reach anyone or be invoked by anyone at any time. When we visualize ourselves immersed in the color of a particular ray, we also draw the higher vibrations of the masters and angelic guardians of that ray into our space.

Below you'll find invocations for each of the rays, so that you can draw in their energies and experience them in your world, and a final activation aligning you with the divine matrix.

The Sapphire Blue Ray

- ©   *Energetic keywords:* Willpower, intention, protection
- ©   *Archangels:* Michael and Faith
- ©   *Divine Masters:* El Morya, Mother Mary

The Sapphire Blue Ray is the energy of truth and of integrity. When we invoke or experience blue energies, we are drawing in pure Source light to help strengthen our will and our intentions.

Invocation

I am one with the Sapphire Blue Ray.
I am aligned with intention and integrity.
I align my will with the highest truth.

The Yellow-Gold Ray

© *Energetic keywords:* Wisdom, illumination, intelligence

© *Archangels:* Uriel, Raguel, Raziel

© *Divine Masters:* Kuthumi

The Yellow-Gold Ray is the energy of wisdom and illumination. When we invoke or experience yellow and gold energies, we are unlocking the infinite intelligence within our soul and uniting with the memories, wisdom, and lessons of all our incarnations.

Invocation

I am one with the Yellow-Gold Ray.
I am aligned with wisdom and intelligence.
I align with illumination and deep knowing.

The Rose Pink Ray

© *Energetic keywords:* Divine love and compassion

© *Archangels:* Gabriel and Hope

© *Divine Masters:* Paul the Venetian and Lady Nada

The Rose Pink Ray of the Heart is the energy of divine love and compassion direct from the heart of Source. When we invoke or experience rose pink energies, we can expect our heart space to transform, opening up to create more space to give and receive love in all shapes and forms.

Invocation

I am one with the Rose Pink Ray.

I am aligned with divine love.

I align my being with infinite compassion and self-care.

The Crystalline Ray

◎ *Energetic keywords:* Clarity, miracles, ascension

◎ *Archangelic beings:* The Holy Spirit and the Shekinah

◎ *Divine Masters:* Serapis Bey, Sanat Kumara, and Lady Venus

The Crystalline Ray, sometimes known as the White Ray, is the energy of clarity, miracles, and ascension. When we invoke or experience crystalline or diamond energies, we can expect inner clarity like never before and a feeling of accelerating along our spiritual path and coming into alignment with the Source of creation.

Invocation

I am one with the Crystalline Ray.

I am one with the miraculous.

I align with divine clarity and the ascended self.

The Emerald Green Ray

◎ *Energetic keywords:* Divine healing and clear vision

◎ *Archangels:* Raphael and Jophiel

◎ *Divine Masters:* Hilarion, Thoth, and Green Tara

The Emerald Green Ray is the energy of divine healing and clear vision. When we invoke or experience emerald green energies, we will experience rapid corrections to old thoughts, patterns, and thinking. This is the ray that initiates healing on all levels, preparing us to become a divine healer through our life on the planet.

Invocation

I am one with the Emerald Green Ray.

I am one with clear vision and perception.

I align with divine healing and infinite awareness.

The Ruby Red Ray

© *Energetic keywords:* Divine awakening, Christ light, heaven on Earth

© *Archangels:* Chamuel, Charity, and the Myriam

© *Divine Masters:* Mary Magdalene and Jesus Christ

The Ruby Red Ray is the energy of divine awakening and Christ light. When we invoke or experience ruby red energies, we are calling up our inner teacher and guide to serve the Earth. This is the ray that encourages us to trust in our light, gifts, and capacity to support healing on a global scale.

Invocation

I am one with the Ruby Red Ray.

I am one with the Christ–Magdalene light.

I awaken the light of heaven on Earth.

The Violet-Purple Ray

© *Energetic keywords:* Divine alchemy, transformation

© *Archangels:* Holy Amethyst and Zadkiel

© *Divine Masters:* Lady Portia and Saint Germain

The Violet-Purple Ray is the energy of divine alchemy and transformation. When we invoke or experience violet-purple energies, we begin to transform all the uncertainty of our life into certainty. This is the energy of divine alchemy, the energy that helps us turn heavy and cumbersome experiences into ones of lightness and joy.

Invocation

I am one with the Violet-Purple Ray.

I am one with divine alchemy.

I align with the energy of transformation.

ACTIVATING THE BRIDGE

Take a deep breath.

Exhale slowly, letting go.

Keep breathing, and with each and every exhale, send your breath earthward through the soles of your feet and connect to the soil.

Imagine an anchor dropping from your heart deep into the heart of Great Mother Earth.

Send a pulse of love from your heart to the Great Mother.

Give thanks for her nourishment.

Be grateful for the planet you call home. Say:

Thank you, Great Mother Earth, for allowing me to be part of you.

Breathe. Sigh. Enjoy your connection to Mother Earth.

Now, every time you inhale, feel yourself reaching upward. Every time you exhale, send your breath skyward.

Feel yourself moving with your breath and rising higher and higher.

Go beyond the clouds. Go into the midnight sky. Reach the stars.

Send a signal from your heart up through your spinal column and the crown of your head to the heart of the universe.

Unite with the One.

Breathe. United. Aligned.

Now that you have connected deeply with the heart of the Earth and the heart of the universe, you are a bridge of light and goodness between the realms, a bridge that is connected to Divine Masters, angels, and beings of light.

Receive wisdom from this connection to divine intelligence.

CHAPTER 6

OPENING UP

'Your angels and guides are as loud as
your willingness to listen.'

A SAYING I OFTEN USE, INSPIRED BY A COURSE IN MIRACLES

We all crave connection. We want to experience it because it's so natural to us. As well as connections through relationships, friendships, and families, we have innate connections to the Earth, the weather, and everything around us. It is our divine right to have a spiritual connection—to connect consciously to the spiritual intelligence of the universe. Not only is this wisdom within the cosmos, it's also within the heart of the Earth and within the heart of our being. How can we access it?

Tuning In

What I've come to understand is that even though we're already connected, in order to experience that connection in a deeper, emotional, visceral way, we have to tune in to it. In most if not all spiritual practices in the world, there is a conscious "tuning in" process that really helps us to step from the ordinary into the extraordinary. Think about the spiritual and religious gatherings, ceremonies, and services you've attended. Remember the simple rituals, prayers, and invocations. These are invitations to enter a state of reflection, to open up and to prepare to listen, to communicate, to connect.

I genuinely believe that our work with the Divine Masters has to be based upon our own individual experience, and I encourage you to create your connection in a way that is authentic and aligned for you. With that being said, I also believe that everything I've learnt from sitting in spiritual circles and having my own spiritual connection for the last 17 years has given me the ability and authority to help others create this connection.

So, back to willingness to listen. I don't think listening is something that can be done instantly. It's going to take practice, and a lot of it. But the more we listen, the more we're going to hear.

I genuinely believe that spiritual beings and guides are excited about connecting to us. They're thrilled that we're down here, walking our spiritual path and intending to live a life of greatness and purpose. They want to support us on this journey, but they're limited by our capacity to hear them and our capacity to ask for help and to welcome it.

Spiritual guidance is basically like one of those answering machines from the nineties. You know the ones that used to have a tape? And to hear the most recent message, you had to sit through every other message that was on the tape before it? If you didn't take care of the older messages, eventually your tape would fill up and there would be no room for new messages. It's often like that when people start spiritual practice. Because we live in such an instantaneous world, where you can order almost anything you want and get it within 24 hours, we expect quick results from meditation, spiritual practice, and even yoga. And if we don't get them, we just move on to something else.

I want to be frank and honest with you. If you've spent a lifetime ignoring the voice you have within, how in heck are you going to hear the voices of Divine Masters? If you want to connect to the masters, first of all you have to listen to yourself. What messages have you been ignoring? You have to dig out that tape of old messages and go through them. Some of the information isn't going to be relevant anymore, and some of it will be stuff you should have dealt with 10 years ago, but a lot will be relevant to where you are right now.

Going through old messages doesn't take forever, but it does require you to show up and acknowledge the messages. Creating a process of regularly checking in and being ready to receive is a wonderful way to begin strengthening the psychic muscles that will allow you to connect with the masters and all the other spiritual beings who are so willing to help you. I've found that taking some time twice a day to really sit and listen in has helped me strengthen my spiritual connection, sharpen my intuitive skills, and become more present in the world.

Messages from the Body

Our body is an intelligent being. It knows how to live and how to heal. It has a natural repair system running at all times. If we cut our finger, our body will do what needs to be done to repair it.

Often our body sends us messages through physical symptoms, emotions, or even intuition. If we've got an upset tummy, for example, and feel that a certain food is causing or adding to the disturbance, we'll steer clear of that food in future—and we'll reap the benefits. If we choose not to listen, and eat that food, we add to our discomfort and we ignore the innate wisdom that rests so deeply within us.

Scanning

A great way to listen to your body is simply by closing your eyes and scanning your physical self.

If there's a part of your body that's uncomfortable, sore, or in need of care, place your hand there (if you can reach) and breathe toward it. In the yogic traditions, there's no difference between the breath and the life-force. The idea is that when you breathe with focus toward a particular part of your being, you bring life-force to it and encourage natural restoration.

Simple steps like this toward self-care and self-service will begin opening up the communication channels within.

Developing Practice

I am privileged to say that I've been able to take part in a number of spiritual practices over the years. I've sat in Spiritualist circles, danced with Wiccan high priestesses, participated in Druid gatherings and shamanic ceremonies, and received initiations from master yogis in India. Most, if not all, of these practices have focused on tuning in and experiencing a shift in consciousness in order to connect with the Divine.

All the methods and practices have enabled my own spiritual practice to develop. When I practiced Ashtanga yoga in Mysore, in southwest India, the classes would begin with hundreds of students chanting in unison, calling in all the masters and teachers of the past to be present with them there. In Kundalini yoga, the opening chant of *"Ong Namo Gurudev Namo"* before any practice is basically saying, "I honor and bow to all that is," and preparing the yogi for their practice. In most shamanic traditions, they'll call the four directions—north, south, east, and west—and the guardians of each direction into every ceremony. It's similar in Wicca and in Celtic traditional practices. Tuning in to and uniting with divine consciousness isn't limited to one lineage or practice, but part of all.

Now that I'm 17 years deep into my own spiritual practice, some things have come and gone, but I will say that I've remained particularly consistent in opening up to listen. I believe this continued willingness has led me to this point and it's why I feel I have the authority to share this work with you now. I'll share my practice with you, but to inspire, not to dictate. Take what resonates, leave what doesn't, and investigate what looks challenging, just in case it's a gateway to opening up like never before.

Here's what I do daily that really helps me to listen out for those divine messages:

© Morning coffee with prayers. I love coffee and I enjoy drinking my coffee in the morning reflecting on my dreams and setting up my intentions for the day.

© Morning yoga practice. Some days it's 20 minutes and light, other days it's 90 minutes and strong. It's purely to listen to my body and what it needs. Afterwards I'll take a 5–10-minute relaxation or meditation.

© Picking an angel or oracle card and reflecting on its message for me.

© Keeping crystals around my desk while I work, checking in with what stone I want to keep close to me that day.

© Evening meditation practice. The first part of this, 11 minutes, is kundalini inspired; the second, 10 minutes, a meditation to listen deeply to the universe. I record my practice and my heart rate on an app.

This is my basic daily practice. It doesn't include working for others. If I'm doing work for or with others, either speaking, leading a workshop, or teaching in some capacity, I'll add in an extra 9–11-minute meditation before I start work, just to set the intention to listen and to hear messages.

Now I know that looks like quite a lot and I'm in the privileged position of working in the spiritual field and having the time and space to do it. Whatever your own situation, if I were to recommend a practice, I'd say morning prayers and listening for five minutes and then a deeper evening meditation practice to wind down. My meditation practice is non-negotiable. That means I can't get out of it, I can't skip it, it's got to happen. Doesn't matter where I am or who I'm with, I'll be doing it, and if that means I'm doing it in the middle of an evening event, I'll be doing it there. If I have friends visiting and it gets to around 10 p.m. and I've still not meditated, I'll say I'm going to do it and the majority will join me in the practice. Meditating with others is called "medidating," ha, ha.

So now we've spoken about my practice, let's start building yours. Here are some important foundational skills to consider. If you already have a spiritual practice, then continue reading, as these suggestions are centered around building psychic connections and opening up so that you can commune with the Divine Masters. They are things I've learnt along the way.

First, let's look at the boundaries I've learnt to put into place so that my experience of spiritual connection is solid, strong, and safe.

Spiritual Protection 101

When you're delving into the spiritual realms, it's always good to have an awareness of how to keep your energy safe and protected. Before your imagination starts running wild, I just want to say that spiritual protection is less about protecting yourself from dark forces and more about just keeping your sensitivity open and ensuring you're not picking up energies that aren't yours. Especially as when you begin to open up to higher dimensions, you become more susceptible to the energies that surround you, and often the energies that aren't yours to carry.

Have you ever walked into a workplace and felt intense anxiety come over you? Or walked into a room and known that someone there isn't in a good mood? Or gone to a hotel for the weekend with a loved one and got the feeling that something strange had happened there? Or had a conversation and walked away feeling the other person had sucked the soul right out of you? That's what you want to protect yourself from—weird vibes that aren't your responsibility, weird vibes that stop you fulfilling your purpose, even weird vibes that you can help with, but don't want to be affected by.

For a long time, I would talk about "putting on my psychic protection," but I was still experiencing sensitivities and being drained by the energies of others. Over the years I've honed my skills and I've come to see that there really is a difference between psychic protection and spiritual protection. Psychic protection is when we're trying to protect ourselves from a lower vibration, and often creating energies that attract challenges in the process, whereas spiritual protection is about inviting a higher power to protect us and not expending our own energy doing so. There really does seem to be a limit to how far our human psyche and energy can go. Believe me, for a long time I was trying to protect myself, when there were spiritual beings and angels who could do it for me.

Having said all this, I still often forget to protect my energy and find myself in situations that feel draining. What I do then is politely say, "Can you please excuse me for a moment? I really need to go to the bathroom." Off to the bathroom I go. I lock myself in a stall, summon my angelic protection, and go back feeling safe and energized.

ANGELIC PROTECTION PROCESS

Here's the most up-to-date, four-step angelic protection process that actually works. It will create an armor of light around you. I based this process on a daily skincare routine. You know the one: the cleanser gets rid of all the muck and grime, exfoliating helps remove anything no longer needed in the surrounding area, the toner firms up the skin, and the moisturizer locks in all of the goodness. You can do exactly the same with your energy.

CLEANSE

First you need to cleanse your energy of any vibes that aren't serving you—anything that's hooked on or attached to you from a challenging conversation, place, or person. There are a couple of ways to do it:

✧   You can imagine sacred fire energy coming from Mother Earth and burning away any unwanted energy that is attached to you. As it touches fear-based energy, it transforms it from fear to love.

✧   You can ask Archangel Michael and his angels to cut the cords of energy that are holding you back or are attached to your energy field with the following prayer:

*Thank you, Archangel Michael and angels of protection, for cutting
the cords that bind me to people, places, energy, situations, and
any other stuff I no longer need.*

It feels so good to know you are here.

I am safe and free!

EXFOLIATE

Exfoliating is all about clearing away any dirt or debris surrounding the
area you are working on. In this case, once you've removed any lower
vibrations or negative cords that are binding you, it's important to invite
angels to clear the space around you. Archangel Metatron is dedicated
to helping remove lower vibrations. He works with sacred geometry to
shift harsh, stagnant energies. You can call upon him to use his magenta
light to clear your space with the following prayer:

*Thank you, Archangel Metatron and angels of sacred geometry, for
clearing the energetic space that surrounds me.*

*Thank you for removing any lower vibrations, blockages, stagnancies,
or anything else that could be standing in the way of love.*

*I welcome your support as you transmute and transform the energy
around me.*

And so it is.

TONE

Toning is all about firming up the goodness that is already there. When
it comes to toning your energy, it's about focusing on a positive aspect of
your present situation, or harnessing a blessing, or choosing to remember
your own worth. Claim your wholeness by declaring that you are
completely in control of your body because it's the vehicle of your soul.
You can say this in your own words, but make sure you are speaking in

the present tense and really putting your foot down. Let the universe and your guides bear witness to the incredible inner strength that you were born with. My favorite declaration is powerful, simple, and effective:

> *I am the keeper of my mind and body.*
>
> *Wherever love is present, fear is a stranger.*
>
> *Love is here!*

When I say, "Love is here," I tap my heart three times, so I can feel a physical response to what I really know deep within me.

MOISTURIZE

When you are moisturizing your energy, you are essentially putting on a coating that you know is going to lock in the goodness. This is the step that everyone knows from books and healing modality trainings, but it won't be truly effective unless the previous steps have been taken. There are a few ways to do it:

✧ You can declare that there is an armor of the holiest light surrounding your whole body and being, extending 10–20 feet (three to six meters) in each direction.

✧ Imagine a cloak of light in the color of your choice swirling all over your body or imagine yourself in a suit of shining armor from head to toe. Again, make sure that the protective light you create radiates out about 10–20 feet (three to six meters) beyond your body in every direction. Really bring that into your vision.

✧ Call on your guides and thank them for protecting you and the energy that surrounds you.

You Are the Keeper of Your Mind and Body

This is a particularly important principle to connect with and embody. It's often said that we're out of control when we're connecting with spiritual energy, but we're not. This is a complete misconception. First of all, I've come to understand, through working with beings of light, that they're always respectful and kind. A lot of these energies are big forces of love, though, and with a lot of love there's the risk of being mentally and emotionally overwhelmed. The reason that connecting with spiritual beings can feel so overwhelming is because the human self is trying to comprehend a spiritual energy from a human perspective. From this perspective, we cannot fully comprehend the energy of the spiritual, and so, when it comes in, it can knock us off our feet. The truth is, this is divine love—a love that is so fiercely loving that all the self-limiting beliefs, ideas, and stories we've learnt along the way are challenged in an instant. This often creates some sort of a healing reaction that allows us to clear out the cobwebs in order to hold more light.

Now, this isn't always practical. We might not have the time or space for it. We might have practical issues to deal with instead. It's important to know that the divine beings we work with respect our Earthly commitments and honor them. If we say at any time that the energy we are feeling is "too much to handle right now," they'll understand and draw back. I've often said something along the lines of "Divine love and spiritual friends I'm connecting with at this time, it genuinely feels so good to know you are here and to feel you like this. Thank you for staying close, but also for ensuring this energy is less intense so that I may operate in the physical realm." They always oblige.

Another concern that many people have when dealing with spiritual energies is the fact that they're not in control and that their body can be "used" in some sense. I think we can thank paranormal movies and television for this.

The truth is, the spiritual realms honor the spiritual law of choice. We have free will, and spiritual beings respect this. Spiritual energies cannot enter our body without an invitation, and even then their energy is subtle, loving, and respectful. There are a lot of stories out there about people being taken over and even speaking in a language that's unknown to them. If you ask me, I find that disrespectful and in some circumstances racist.

That's not going to happen to you when you connect to the Divine Masters. They are your friends and spiritual allies. They want to help you process this realm and move into a heightened state of being. Their energy will support you, not put you in any circumstances that will challenge you physically.

So, if ever you feel overwhelmed when spiritual energy comes close to you, know you are in control of the situation. You are the keeper of your mind and body. This is your vehicle, you are in the driving seat and right next to you is Source/God/Whatever you'd like to call it. Just do what I do if ever spiritual energy feels overwhelming to me. I simply treat it the same way I would treat someone who got too close for my comfort on the physical plane: I use the authority of my voice and heart to hold space for myself and say: "You're too close for comfort. Thank you for stepping back." They *must* honor this.

In moments that feel intense on a spiritual level, I also call back my power with the words I use when "toning." You will remember them:

I am the keeper of my mind and body.
Wherever love is present, fear is a stranger.
Love is here!

And again, when I say, "Love is here!" I tap my heart. It really helps me embody my power.

Use Discernment

Developing the capacity to connect with the wisdom of masters, guides, and angels comes down to being able to discern who is doing the talking. We all have a voice of infinite intelligence within us, but we also have a voice that is limiting, fear-based, and challenging to deal with: the ego.

One way that I've been able to overcome the limitations of my ego voice is by making peace with it. For a long time, I tried to fight "her" off (because for some reason I picture my ego as Karen from the TV show *Will and Grace*), but I've realized that as soon as I try to fight with my ego, I create a war within my own mind. So, instead of pushing her away, I acknowledge her. The way we become One is by eliminating all third parties.

Over the years I've also found a particularly simple way to determine who is doing the talking—any talking—just by how the conversation is flowing. Now, I want you to know that often spiritual beings and guides, including masters and angels, will speak to you through your own inner voice. This inner voice is the master within. We'll meet that master later in this book. You can call them Christ consciousness, the inner teacher, or even the inner buddha. Whatever you want to call them, they're there, and they are the vehicle the masters will often use in order to communicate.

The best way to determine who is doing the talking is by checking in with how you feel. This is why listening to the body is so useful. If you're feeling agitated, overwhelmed, or even angry, it's most certainly your ego talking. The ego is annoyed, angry, furious even, bitchy, limiting, and always in a rush. When your ego is speaking, your jaw will clench, your ass will clench, and you'll feel uptight, scared, insecure, and small. The ego always operates in linear time–space and fears consequences, for example, "If you don't do this, something bad will happen."

When divine intelligence is speaking, everything is calm. Even if you are in the most stressful circumstances, there will be a feeling of peace. The voice of love is peaceful, calm, cool, determined, collected, determined, present, firm, and fair. When divine love comes through with a message, it always trusts in the greater unfolding. Even if you're in a life-or-death situation, it will be peaceful, calm, and collected when it's speaking, and you will feel this energy wash over you too.

You have a choice in every moment and every message. My prayer is that this information will help you decode the spiritual connections you are making.

CHAPTER 7

SPIRITUAL ALIGNMENT

*"Align with the light of the whole universe
and all uncertainty will fall away."*

THE EMERALD TABLET

Creating a sense of alignment within our energy is essential to building connections and relationships with the Divine Masters. Everything in the entire universe is comprised of energy, and that includes us and the cosmic spiritual guides who are on standby, waiting for us to call them in. With that being said, energy vibrates at different frequencies.

Vibration and Frequency

We've actually already explored vibration and frequency when looking at spiritual protection. Even when we're not intentionally being intuitive, we can experience the natural fluctuations of energy around us. Have you ever been somewhere and got a strange vibe about it, then discovered that something devastating happened there? Or sensed that someone wasn't themselves and found out they'd recently had some sad news? We are all energetic barometers reading the energy around us. It's our nature to receive information on a vibrational level.

But not only are we receiving and experiencing energy, we are expressing it too. Sometimes *we* are the person giving off the strange vibe, or the person it's draining to be around, and it's not because we're negative people, it's simply because we're people. We experience a range of emotions and our vibration fluctuates. It's important to learn how to raise our vibration and also how to retune our energy when we're hitting a vibrational low. Why?

Energy Is Attractive

Energy is an attractive force—it draws other energies to it. Matching energies. We know that to be true from human relationships. We'll find ourselves attracting friends who are often similarly minded, for example. It works both ways: we'll also find that the company we keep influences our language, ideas, and beliefs. Sometimes our friendship circles will change if we find ourselves opening up to new ideas. There will no longer be common ground, or the right "vibe," and we'll find ourselves moving on and attracting new friendships.

When it comes to experiencing the energy of Divine Masters, angels, and other spiritual beings, we simply want to shift our vibration so that we become more open to divine experiences. We want to raise our vibration. It's really important to clear the energetics around the moments when we're not feeling ourselves or are having a bad day. These are okay! We all have them, and having a challenging moment doesn't push away angels or stop us developing our divine connection. It doesn't work like that. But it's best to move through these moments. I believe that's the only way to overcome them. I've also come to understand that sometimes, in our lowest moments, angels and Divine Masters can come through. So, if you've had challenges in your mental or emotional wellbeing, know that you can still develop a bond with these spiritual guides, even though you just might find that when you're feeling more upbeat, excited, and energetic, it will be easier to access their messages.

Human energetics are like a wave—they come and they go. One moment we can be happy, the next moment we can be sad. There are moments when we're filled with frustration, envy, grief, and goodness knows what else, and moments we feel unstoppable, excited, and fulfilled. We feel all the emotions, and that's the key: to feel them. As I said before, in order to hear Divine Masters, we have to be willing to hear ourselves too.

Vibration Is Magnetic

Energy vibrates, so it's no surprise that vibration is magnetic, and we draw vibrations to us that match those we're sending out. Louise Hay would say, "How you start your day is how you live your day," and it's true. We use other phrases to describe this, such as "I got out the wrong side of bed today" when things are going wrong or from bad to worse. Instinctively, we know when something is off. We know when we're vibrating high too! "As high as a kite," as the saying goes. Some days it feels as though the stars have aligned just for us and everything is falling into place. This is a high vibration, and we can cultivate it.

Choosing to align to the highest vibration possible helps us develop our spiritual awareness and ultimately aligns us to the energy of creation. In fact, the creation story in Hinduism, one of the oldest spiritual traditions in the world, relates that in the beginning there was sound. That sound was "OM," a pulsing vibrational energy that carried across the land and began to create life. That vibration is within us all to this day, and we can maintain it and direct it.

Over the years, I've found that it's in the moments when my vibration is the highest that I have the most poignant spiritual experiences. It's for this reason that I make it my daily practice to consciously move into higher vibrational states. Like everyone, I do fluctuate. But knowing that state is there and I can move into it is so reassuring to me. The other thing—an "off" moment—doesn't make me feel any less spiritual, and I certainly don't use it as a way to self-loathe. In fact, I know it is a call for *love* and an opportunity to care for my needs even more than usual.

Ways to Raise Our Vibration

What I've found is that in the moments that we're not feeling ourselves, we can call in help to make that shift back to a higher vibration. If we open up to the love that surrounds us, it will enter our being. In fact it's at moments like this that we really benefit from our spiritual connection.

We can raise our vibration in other ways too:

© *Spending time in nature:* Going for a walk in nature, chilling at the beach, and going barefoot on the earth or sand are all great ways to reset our energy and our frequency.

© *Moving our body:* Exercise, dance, and yoga are all known for their capacity to increase endorphins and induce a feeling of wellbeing. These are great ways to rise up!

© *Indulging in self-care:* A nice bath, some personal grooming, and/or a facial, pedicure, or other beauty treatment are all great ways to shift our awareness toward ourselves and feel good.

© *Meditating and doing breath work:* Taking time to meditate and breathe allows us to peel away any layers of resistance that have built up inside us, lower our shields, and let love in.

© *"Showering off" the day:* Most people feel better after a shower. While in the shower, why not imagine the water washing away any lower vibrations or energies that could be standing between you and joy?

© *Feeling grateful:* Counting our blessings will allow our heart to open and our vibration to rise.

© *Touching and connecting:* Spending time with others, holding hands, cuddling, and making love are also great ways to raise our frequency.

And now, more alignment...

Chakra Alignment

Chakra is a Sanskrit word that means "wheel" and is used to describe an energy center of the body. The idea is that there are many of these centers, all linking to different aspects of the body, mind, and soul. In traditional yogic teaching there are seven main ones in a vertical line up the spine, starting at the base and running all the way up to the crown of the head. Pure primal life-force energy moves up the spine in two streams of energy known as Ida (feminine/lunar energy) and Pingala (masculine/solar). They crisscross each other at points on a central channel, the Sushumna channel, and form a vortex of energy every time they cross. The vortices are the chakras.

According to Tantric philosophy, there is also a primal spiritual energy known as kundalini, which means "coiled snake," at the base of our spine. In most of us, this sacred serpent power is lying dormant. According to the Tantras, the spiritual texts of the Hindu, Buddhist, and Jain traditions, when we begin spiritual practice, it will begin to uncoil and move up through our chakras, helping us reach a state of heightened awareness in preparation for *samadhi*/ascension.

This is our spiritual anatomy. Our chakras are little vortices that are bringing energy in and feeding our intuition, and then our intuition is sending signals and processing emotions accordingly.

Our chakras are influenced by our environment, our beliefs, and any other energies we come into contact with. An awareness of our chakra alignment gives us a road map to personal mastery—and to powerful relationships with Divine Masters and other spiritual guides.

Just like our body, our chakras need tender loving care. They can spiral out of alignment if one particular energy is dominant and become muted or clogged up if there's an energy that is draining us. From my own experience, it's very rare for a chakra to be completely blocked, but quite common for one to be "leaking" energy, in the sense that it's feeding a situation that's not in our best interest.

To have a clear, visceral, and internal connection with the Divine Masters, it's essential for us to have our chakras in alignment. When they are in alignment, we create a bridge of light between this realm and the next. We let the kundalini energy within us rise up, and ultimately that opens up energetic space for us to reach our full spiritual potential and connect with the ancient wisdom of the universe.

Raising our vibration through spiritual practice will ultimately bring our chakras into balance. If you have a strong meditation practice, regularly bringing light through your spinal column is a great way to ensure your chakras are in alignment.

Here's a breakdown of the chakras, the energies they represent, and affirmations to bring them back into alignment. As you read through the list, it's important to assess if you've had any challenges with any of the key topics that these energy centers represent. If one seems to stick out or you want to develop strength in that part of your body or area of your life, then that is the energetic space that's calling for your attention. If you work with the affirmations here before using an activation to connect with a master (*in Part III*), I can guarantee you'll have a clearer experience.

Base Chakra

- © *Location:* Tip of the tail bone, lower back
- © *Name:* Muladhara, "Root Support"
- © *Color:* Red
- © *Element:* Earth
- © *Key energetic topics:* Safety, security, home, family
- © *Representing:* Our right to be here on the planet. In nature, the base chakra would be the soil in which seeds are planted.
- © *Physiology:* The lower half of the body, legs, feet, base of the spine, and lower discs
- © *Suggested crystals:* Stones that are black, smoky, brown, or red

Affirmations to breathe in:

I have a right to be here on Earth.
I have chosen to incarnate on this planet.
It is safe for me to be here.

Sacral Chakra

- © *Location:* Below the navel, at the top of the pubic bone, the sacrum
- © *Name:* Svadisthana, "One's own place"
- © *Color:* Orange

- *Element:* Water

- *Key energetic topics:* Flow, trust in life, the capacity to create, produce, and reproduce

- *Representing:* Our right to be in our own body. In nature, the sacral chakra would be the water that feeds the soil for seeds to grow.

- *Physiology:* The reproductive system, sexual organs

- *Suggested crystals:* Stones that are orange, golden, or brown

Affirmations to breathe in:

My body is the home of my soul.
I have a right to be in my body.
I am safe in my body.

Solar Plexus Chakra

- *Location:* The center of the belly (above the navel)

- *Name:* Manipura, "Lustrous Gem"

- *Color:* Yellow

- *Element:* Fire

- *Key energetic topics:* Willpower, drive, intention, decisions

- *Representing:* Our right to decide. In nature, the solar plexus would be the sun that kisses the soil and encourages seeds to germinate and grow.

- *Physiology:* The stomach, digestive system, central organs, intestines, middle back, core muscles

- *Suggested crystals:* Stones that are yellowish, clear yellow, golden, orange, and clear with gold/yellow/red

Affirmations to breathe in:

I have a right to make my own decisions.

My will is strong and focused.

It is safe for me to manifest the life I desire.

Heart Chakra

◎ *Location:* Center of the chest

◎ *Name:* Anahata, "Unstruck"

◎ *Color:* Green/pink

◎ *Element:* Air

◎ *Key energetic topics:* Giving love, receiving love, compassion, altruism, service

◎ *Representing:* Our right to love and be loved. In nature, the heart chakra would be the air/wind supporting the bees and therefore pollination.

◎ *Physiology:* The heart, upper respiratory tract, chest, breasts, middle back, sternum

◎ *Suggested crystals:* Stones that are any shade of green, also aquamarine, pink, or clear with pink or green

Affirmations to breathe in:

I have a right to love and be loved.

My heart is open to giving and receiving.

It is safe for me to accept love.

Throat Chakra

- *Location:* Throat/neck
- *Name:* Vishuddha, "the Purifier"
- *Color:* Blue
- *Element:* Space/Akasha
- *Key energetic topics:* Expression, the voice, speaking up, truth
- *Representing:* Our right to express ourselves, speak up, share our truth, and be heard. In nature, the throat chakra would be the life-force that flowers need in order to open and express themselves.
- *Physiology:* The throat, shoulders, upper chest, thyroid, hormonal flow
- *Suggested crystals:* Stones that are any shade of blue, aquamarine, clear with blue

Affirmations to breathe in:

I have a right to speak my truth and be heard.
I express myself with openness and honesty.
It is safe for me to express my authentic self.

Brow (Third Eye) Chakra

- *Location:* Between the brows
- *Name:* Ajna, "Perception"
- *Color:* Indigo/deep purple
- *Element:* Space/Akasha

- *Key energetic topics:* Inner vision, imagination, perception, perspective
- *Representing:* Our right to see on a physical and spiritual level. In nature, the brow chakra would be the spirit that lets flowers express their individual beauty.
- *Physiology:* The eyes, head space, frontal lobes of the brain
- *Suggested crystals:* Stones that are deep blue, purple, or violet

Affirmations to breathe in:

I have a right to see the world through my own eyes.

I awaken and trust my inner vision.

It is safe for me to see and be seen.

Crown Chakra

- *Location:* At the top of the head
- *Name:* Sahasrara, "Thousand petaled," referring to a lotus
- *Color:* Violet/crystal clear
- *Element:* Light
- *Key energetic topics:* Spiritual connection, mental connection, how we see/experience God
- *Representing:* Our right to experience the Divine. In nature, the crown chakra would be the essence that gives the natural world a purpose.
- *Physiology:* The crown of the head, brain, the upper head, hair/scalp
- *Suggested crystals:* Stones that are violet, clear, or rainbow-colored

Affirmations to breathe in:

I have a right to know the Divine.

I accept that I am part of the bigger picture.

It is safe for me to connect with spirit.

Most people have heard of these seven chakras, but there are four others that are being rediscovered and accessed in spiritual circles nowadays. Supposedly there are even more, but these 11 (seven traditional and four "new") are the ones I work with. Here are the new ones:

Earth Star Chakra

- *Location:* 6–12 inches (15–30 cm) below the feet
- *Color:* Copper/bronze
- *Element:* All the new chakras are fourth-dimensional, so beyond elements.
- *Key energetic topics:* Connection with the Earth, the wisdom of the Earth, groundedness, a sense of belonging
- *Representing:* Our right to be on the Earth. Our Earth Star chakra allows us to connect directly with the Earth Mother (Gaia) and her angels.
- *Suggested crystals*: Golden, brown, smoky quartz, copper- or metallic-covered stones

Affirmations to breathe in:

I connect deeply with the heart of the Earth.

I have a right to know Earthly wisdom.

It is safe for me to walk the planet and live with purpose.

Soul Star Chakra

○ *Location:* 6–12 inches (15–30 cm) above the head

○ *Color:* Magenta/crystalline

○ *Key energetic topics:* Soul connection, higher purpose, connection to divine wisdom

○ *Representing:* Our right to know our soul's purpose. Our Soul Star allows us to connect directly with the Sky Father/the universe and the angels of ancient wisdom.

○ *Suggested crystals/metals:* Ruby, rutilated or Lemurian quartz, "aura" crystals, platinum

Affirmations to breathe in:

I have a right to know my soul's purpose.

I connect deeply with the I AM Presence (see below).

It is safe for me to receive and connect with ancient wisdom.

Stellar Gateway Chakra

○ *Location:* 12 inches (30 cm) or more above the head

○ *Color:* Beyond color—looks like a Milky Way of stars

○ *Key energetic topics:* Connection to Source, star power, remembering our cosmic origin

○ *Representing:* Our right to remember our cosmic origin. Our Stellar Gateway allows us to connect directly with the God particle.

○ *Suggested crystals:* Any crystal that looks like stars or the night sky, obsidian, Lemurian seeds, moldavite, Libyan desert glass, meteor pieces, euclase

Affirmations to breathe in:

I have a right to remember my cosmic origin.

I connect deeply with the power of the cosmos.

It is safe for me to remember, manifest, and create.

Gaia Gateway Chakra

◎ *Location:* 12 inches (30 cm) or more below the feet

◎ *Color:* Deep brown and black with hints of copper

◎ *Key energetic topics:* Connection to Gaia and the inner Earth, the matrix of early consciousness; also Earth power, remembering past lives

◎ *Representing:* Our right to remember our divine mission or purpose. Our Gaia Gateway allows us to connect directly with the Earth's intelligence/ divine matrix.

◎ *Suggested crystals:* Any stone that's black, brown, copper, or gold. Crystal skulls connect directly to this chakra.

Affirmations to breathe in:

I have a right to incarnate in this dimension.

The Earth is my loving mother.

It is safe for me to be at home on Gaia.

The I AM Presence

"The Mighty I AM Presence" is frequently mentioned in the Ascended Master teachings. It's defined as the individualized presence of the Divine that rests within us all. Personally, I see no difference between the I AM

Presence and what other people might call the inner teacher or higher self. It's the aspect of divinity that lies within us, offering us great wisdom. It's the inner buddha or Christ consciousness. Bringing it to the forefront of our mind will also help our spiritual alignment.

Throughout this book I work with the power of I AM—it's in most of the activations and prayers shared here. When we use the words "I AM," we are quite literally bringing the frequencies of the words that follow into our being. This is why positive affirmations can bring about huge shifts.

"The I AM-ness," as I often call it, is ultimately an inner Divine Master who's ready and willing to be activated. When we call on this presence, we begin to align with the light and receive information that will support our growth.

Not only that, as like attracts like, according to the laws of the universe, the light that begins to radiate from the core of our being will begin to draw other sources of light, including masters, angels, and other cosmic light beings. How great is that?

The only way to really learn about the I AM Presence is to experience it. Try it now.

Connect with the I AM Presence

Place one hand on your belly, one hand on your heart. Breathe.

Visualize an incredible light in the core of your being. See this light growing brighter and brighter. Let it cover your entire human self.

See it shining up and out.

Within you, imagine an incredible golden light reaching up and out to connect with the universal life-force. See it aligning with the light of greatness held within the cosmos.

Become one with the cosmos, accessing the divine matrix, aligning with the divine mind.

Breathe in. Breathe out. Connected.

Say:

> *I am one with the light.*
>
> *I am united and one with the light.*
>
> *I am aligned and connected to the Source of light.*
>
> *I am the created and the creator.*
>
> *I am all that is, was, and ever will be.*
>
> *I call forth, from the core of my being, the Mighty I AM Presence.*
>
> *Great universal cosmonaut, star being, star power, thank you for standing at the forefront of my heart and mind.*
>
> *Thank you for leading the way with your divine intelligence.*
>
> *Thank you, Universal Source, for sending your holy masters and angels of light to guide me.*
>
> *I am one with infinite intelligence.*
>
> *I am one infinite possibility.*
>
> *I am surrounded by the light.*
>
> *I am guided by the light.*
>
> *I am the light.*
>
> *I am the light.*
>
> *I am the light.*

PART III

WORKING WITH THE MASTERS

Divine Masters, keepers of ancient wisdom.

Thank you for shining your infinite light upon my being
and for helping me access the teacher I have within.

I am ready to unlock my gifts.

I am willing to experience you.

I open myself up to you.

And so it is.

CHAPTER 8

THE ACTIVATION PROCESS

*"If you want to find the secrets of the universe,
think in terms of energy, frequency, and vibration."*

NIKOLA TESLA

Spiritual energy resides within us all. It is unborn and therefore it will never die. It's the part of us that came from the heart of the cosmos and the part that will return when our mortal body has completed its time here. The masters have helped me realize that this "eternal-ness" that resides within us all is actually still present in the heart of Source. Our human life is something of a hologram. What we see and what we experience are very real, but the ultimate truth is that we have never left the heart of Source.

With that being said, many of us have forgotten our spiritual truth and our spiritual power. But the fact that you're here right now, connecting to the masters and their wisdom, shows that a deep awakening is happening within. For many of us, our spiritual power is on the rise. It's coming forth and we are remembering our divine origins.

For me, crystal skulls have been great teachers, and it's through working with these mysterious ancient beings (remember that even if the carving is new, the crystal is ancient) that I've learnt that, just like them, we have energies within us that can be activated. I like to think that all the wisdom of our cosmic self is just waiting to be called on, through the stargate of our heart space. It's waiting to be activated.

As I was preparing to write this book, I came into the awareness that the Divine Masters have activations to share.

What Is an Activation?

An activation is a process of awakening a spiritual energy within our being. The idea is that a powerful intentional prayer, combined with visualization and spiritual ceremony, calls forth, from the heart of our being, energies that can support our spiritual development and prepare us for ascension.

Even if activation doesn't seem a natural process to you, or isn't something you've ever given any thought to, through the divine matrix, that infinite connection with the everything that is and ever will be, you have the power of the universe within you and you can experience it in a personal way in this lifetime.

What Can an Activation Do?

Activations ultimately create more space for light and miracles in our life. Even though these intentional prayers are about awakening something that is lying dormant within, they also draw in and attune us to frequencies that will support our human experience. They open up energetic space for us to be surrounded by divine beings and masters who want to assist us on our journey. When we begin to activate spiritual energies in this way, anything contrasting or unsupportive within our being will begin to shift and heal. Activations are ultimately psychic processes that shift and retune our energy, so we are in alignment with our greatest good and the highest intelligence available to us.

How to Get the Best from an Activation

Follow Your Intuition

By following the call of your intuition, you will be drawn to work with the Divine Masters who can best serve you and your personal journey. You may want to work your way through these 33 Divine Masters and their activations in order, or you may feel drawn to working with a particular master over a period of time.

Activations don't have to be one-time experiences—you can revisit them regularly and often. The more you connect with a master's activation, the more you will unlock and remember on a spiritual, cosmic level.

Be Open to New Information

When you're working through an activation or "processing" the experience afterwards, it's important to stay open to information that comes to you and through you. You may find yourself thinking about a particular person, or a situation in your past, or even a previous incarnation. Whatever it is, stay open, stay aware, and stay connected. I've found that keeping a loose journal has been very helpful. It's not something I do every day, but writing down the impressions, messages, and ideas that come to me has been very useful. Over the years I have looked back through my journal and found a lot of pivotal pieces of information that I've taken out and shared with the world.

Remember This Is a Joyous Experience

When you're working with activation energy, remember that this is a joyous experience. You are remembering and uniting with Divine Masters and cosmic information. These connections are going to help you become a more ascended and aware human being. Lightness attracts light, so don't enter the space grumpy or when you are feeling stuck, just raise your vibration (*see p.82*) and then move into the space of energy and ceremony with a light heart.

Tips for the Journey

© Schedule regular time for spiritual practice. The more you show up, the more the light will show up for you.

© If you're out and about while integrating a particular master's activation and you can't take your book with you to refer back to, it might be worth taking a copy of the activation prayer so you can re-center yourself or align with the energy whenever you need to.

© Connect with the energy of your chakras (*see p.83*) when working with Divine Masters and see which ones strengthen your connection.

© Share your experiences with your friends or a teacher on the spiritual path. It's always good to process your experiences with someone else who's connected.

© Be open to experiencing things differently. Know that there is a gift in experiencing things in your own unique way.

COMMANDER ASHTAR

Commander Ashtar, also known as Ashtar, is a multi-dimensional extraterrestrial who promotes truth, peace, and harmony between planets. Although essentially an "alien," this divine cosmic being is known to appear in human form so that he can communicate at a heart level with those on Earth who are feeling called to connect with interplanetary beings and starships. He is the leader and guide of the Star Command, a congregation of extraterrestrial beings who are dedicated to the protection and guardianship of the Earth. In modern-day spirituality, it has become accepted that Commander Ashtar is part of the Great White Brotherhood (*see p.33*) and is the divine intermediary between this planet/dimension and others.

He was first introduced to the world in 1952, through the work of a man named George Van Tassel, who was a founding father of ufology. Van Tassel claimed he was receiving telepathic communications from Ashtar. Since then, Ashtar has become a strong point of contact for people who are interested in UFOs and inter-dimensional communication, essentially becoming one of the first ever cosmic superstars of our time.

Meeting the Star Command

Ever since I was little, I've had a deep knowing that we're not the only form of life in this universe. But, though I've always had a natural spiritual connection with the afterlife and angels, the thought of connecting with extraterrestrials somewhat unnerved me. I had a very strong connection to the stars, and the movie *ET* created quite an emotional reaction in me, but when I first started to learn about Ashtar, I was hesitant to connect.

I remember receiving a download about this some years ago when I was reading about multi-dimensional connection. It was just very clear guidance that settled me instantly. I realized that the real reason I was hesitant to connect with cosmic beings was because in a previous incarnation, I was one. So, I was unconsciously concerned that if I contacted cosmic beings, I might not feel settled here anymore and might long for "home." Thankfully, this isn't something I have felt, but I know it is experienced by many incarnated starpeople.

That night I dreamed I was transported to the Star Command. I found myself on a starship with humanoid beings wearing high-necked grandad-collared blue, purple, and golden uniforms, similar to those in *Star Trek*. Many had long, flowing hair, while others had shaved heads and golden-colored markings on their foreheads. They had skin shades of all colors, similar to the human race. I remember knowing that this starship didn't exist physically in this realm, but in a higher dimension. It seemed that this energetic space was dedicated to the protection of planet Earth.

I remember Ashtar appearing in the dream. He looked just like a normal man, but was very tall. He had long, flowing blond hair and creamy white skin. The only thing that made him really stand out were his light gray eyes. They were very bright and definitely otherworldly, almost angelic.

Commander Ashtar will be your guide and guardian so that you can experience extraterrestrial connection in a way that is safe and guarded. If you feel you've made contact with an alien life-force or seen a UFO, you can call on him and his command to enlighten you on the experience.

He also helps lightworkers take the necessary steps to fulfill their divine purpose. He encourages us all to lead by example, take charge of our life mission, and walk our talk. If you are feeling held back or frustrated, Ashtar can give you an extraterrestrial kick in the butt to get you moving along your spiritual path.

Working with Commander Ashtar

Working with Commander Ashtar and the Star Command can help you with:

© understanding UFO and alien experiences

© establishing connections beyond this dimension

© overcoming your longing for a distant home, if you feel you were a starperson previously

© stepping onto your path and leading by example

Commander Ashtar's activation is an intentional prayer to call the light up from within so it can lead the way.

LEADER OF LIGHT ACTIVATION

Breathe deeply. Reach upward through your crown, Soul Star, and Stellar Gateway chakras.

Imagine that you are sending a signal of light into the sky and connecting with a giant starship in the center of the cosmos.

When you feel connected, be open to receiving downloads of information.

When you're ready, say this prayer:

> *Commander Ashtar, Star Command, interplanetary beings of love,*
> *Thank you for blessing me with your cosmic starlight.*
> *I welcome your presence and your connection into my heart space at this time.*
> *Thank you for unlocking my awareness of my gifts, strengths, and unique qualities, so that I can step onto the path of purpose with focus and intention.*
> *Thank you, Commander Ashtar, for becoming a leader and guide to me, so that I can become a leader and guide to all those who require motivation, inspiration, and direction.*
> *I welcome your high-frequency healing downloads, unique information, and cosmic codes, so that I can align to the path of service and support the greater healing of the world.*
> *Thank you for sending me a gentle sign of your presence and for helping me form and strengthen my starry connection so that I can tap into the cosmic light of my soul.*
> *It feels so good to know your guiding presence is with me now.*
> *I am one with the Star Command.*
> *I am blessed to experience their presence.*
> *And so it is.*

MAHAVATAR BABAJI

Mahavatar Babaji, also known simply as Babaji, is a master yogi and the carrier of the Christ light in India. He was introduced to the world through the much-cherished book *Autobiography of a Yogi* by Paramahansa Yogananda.

In Sanskrit the word *maha* means "great," *avatar* means "descent," and *babaji* is "father" or "grandfather." Mahavatar Babaji, therefore, is Great Incarnated Father. In Hindu culture, it is widely believed that an avatar is an incarnation of a deity or divine being.

A Yogi from 2,000 Years Ago

According to the work of Paramahansa Yogananda, Mahavatar Babaji was born in AD 203 in a small coastal village in Tamil Nadu, India. His birth name was Nagaraj, which means "Serpent King"—a reference to the kundalini energy we all have within (*see p.83*). When he was just 15, he went on a spiritual quest that led him to be initiated into ancient yogic practices, including Kriya yoga (cleansing) and Pranayama (yogic breathing techniques). From there, he went on into the Himalayas, to delve deeply into spiritual studies and ultimately to become a *siddha*, which is a yogic term for a perfected being, similar to a buddha.

The story goes that Mahavatar Babaji went on an inner and outer journey to discover the sacred power of yoga. Yoga is ultimately the mental, physical, and emotional practice of uniting spirit and body. Through his practice, this young soul became so entranced by and connected to the divine life-force that surrounded him, it is said he was nourished by divine light alone. He completely detached from his ego, allowed pure light to reach into his being on a cellular level, and so transcended life and death. He decided, however, to remain on the Earth plane to be a great teacher to all those who called on him, especially those wanting to achieve unification through yoga.

Mahavatar Babaji ascended as a young man, so when I see him clairvoyantly, he looks youthful, with long, flowing hair, dark brown skin and deep brown eyes that pierce my soul. He appears in just a simple loincloth. Light radiates from him.

Babaji helps us connect with the infinite presence and light of God, so that we can really know on a heart level that we are part of a divine plan. He is said to take full human form and then move back to spiritual form at will. He has a hidden temple in the Himalayas and this sacred space will appear to adepts and wandering yogis when they are ready to be initiated into the ancient ways.

Yogananda shared that in his "lost years," Jesus Christ went on a soul journey of his own and connected with Mahavatar Babaji, who initiated him into Kriya yoga and shared yogic wisdom and practices with him. Although there's no way to prove this, it does make you think. Indian *siddhas* are impressive people—they can lie on beds of nails and overcome pain, and they're even said to be able to levitate. Maybe Jesus Christ was able to walk on water and endure the pain of the crucifixion because he was a master of yogic breathing. Something to feel into.

Paramahansa Yogananda says:

The Mahavatar is in constant communion with Christ; together they send out vibrations of redemption and have planned the spiritual technique of salvation for this age. The work of these two fully illumined masters—one with the body, and one without it—is to inspire the nations to forsake suicidal wars, race hatreds, religious sectarianism, and the boomerang-evils of materialism.

Working with Babaji

Working with Babaji can:

◎ help you on the yogic journey

◎ help you unite body, mind, and soul

◎ support you in establishing a clear connection to the Divine

◎ help you embody the Christ light on Earth

Mahavatar Babaji's activation is a life-replenishing one that allows you to draw down pure consciousness and awaken the Christ light in your heart.

Cosmic Expansion Activation

Visualize yourself in pure golden light, then say these words:

Mahavatar Babaji, ancient yogi, master of the Christ light,

Thank you for downloading your sacred teachings and wisdom into my being.

Thank you for transporting me to the hidden temples of the Himalayas so I can receive the replenishing light of the cosmos.

I welcome the Christ light into my being to activate my kundalini energy, reconfigure my frequency.

Christ light, unite with my body.

Christ light, unite with my mind.

Christ light, unite with my soul.

I AM united with the energy of pure consciousness.

I AM filled with infinite light and prana.

I allow my being and soul to expand.

And so it is.

BRIGID

B rigid (sometimes spelled Brigit) is a Celtic goddess of Ireland who is closely associated with fire and the season of spring. Her name means "the bright one" and she is the goddess of fertility, healing, and all the renewing energies that spring brings. She is the protector of wells and holy shrines throughout Ireland.

Brigid was so loved by the Irish people that when Christianity came to the country, the Catholic Church adopted her as a saint. St Brigid is now the saint of babies, farmers, cows, and anything associated with living off the land.

Brigid is a powerful goddess who can help us channel our energy into something that is important for our growth. As she is a divine figure who has lasted through the ages and been able to transcend the limitations of religious dogma, she adds longevity to our journey so that we can reach a deep state of wholeness.

Goddess of Fire

Brigid appears as a beautiful Irishwoman. She has long fiery red hair and wears an emerald green robe. In her hands she cups a sacred flame—the energy of fire in which she governs. She has a soft spot for those who live and work on the Earth. Those who are interested in paganism, Wicca, or any other Earth-based spiritual practice will feel called to her.

The Celtic festival of Imbolc, celebrated around February 2nd in the northern hemisphere and August 2nd in the southern hemisphere, is sacred to Brigid's energy. It's the time of the "first milk," when the first lambs and calves are born. It's a time of new beginnings and looking forward, for summer is coming, with its abundance, harvest, and reward. Traditional pagan practitioners will often light a fire at Imbolc as a symbol of warmth returning to the land.

On a spiritual and energetic level, fire symbolizes purification. Working with Brigid, you can call on her to send her sacred flames your way. This fiery energy can burn away anything that's not serving you and bring the blessings of fertility, new beginnings, new projects, and growth. When you feel called to connect with Brigid, your own spiritual fire is rising within. She comes with the message that your power is greater than you may think.

Brigid helps us take an inventory of our life and recognize how far we have come on our journey. Through connecting with her essence, we connect with our inner fire, that powerful force that helps us embrace our passions and make any changes needed in order to be our most authentic self.

Fertility Goddess

As Brigid is strongly associated with spring and the first milk, she is also strongly associated with fertility and motherhood. There is something sacred about motherhood and it is a time when a woman steps into the wholeness of her power.

Brigid is a powerful guide for women who are finding it difficult to embrace their womanhood or struggling to find and unite with their power. She is also an amazing support if you would like guidance on conception and giving birth to new life, of whatever kind.

Working with Brigid

Working with Brigid can:

© help you connect with your passions and desires

© give you support with fertility and giving birth to new projects

© guide you to connect with Celtic ancestry and the people of those lands

© ignite your inner fire

Brigid's activation is an energetic awakening of your inner fire. This is held in the solar plexus chakra, the energetic space that deals with your capacity to exert your will and fulfil your desires.

INNER FIRE ACTIVATION

Breathe deeply.

Bring your left hand to your solar plexus and allow your right hand to overlap it.

If you've detached from a desire or a deep need in your life, think of it now.

If there are parts of your inner truth that you've felt disconnected from, remember them now.

When you're ready, say this prayer:

> *Great Celtic goddess Brigid, saint of the land, mother of wells and holy places, thank you for embracing me with your holy love.*
>
> *O bright one, fill up the vessel of my being with your burning bright light.*
>
> *Thank you for helping me connect with my capacity to create.*
>
> *Thank you for helping me locate the aspects of my being that are filled with passion and drive.*
>
> *Thank you for helping me share my gifts and my true self with the world.*
>
> *I am embraced by your light.*
>
> *I give permission for my passions and desires to be ignited.*
>
> *Sacred fire within, burn brightly.*
>
> *O holy goddess, thank you for warming my heart with your presence as I step onto the path of truth once more.*
>
> *And so it is.*

MASTER BUDDHA

The Buddha or Master Buddha, also known as Gautama Buddha or Siddhartha, is the main figure of Buddhism, a prince turned enlightened being, who lived in India around the fifth century BCE. Revered the world over as a figure of peace, he has become a role-model, guiding figure, and great teacher to the spiritual, religious, and even just curious.

Born a prince, Siddhartha, he initially lived a protected life behind the closed gates of the palace. It is said that at his birth a wise sage predicted that he would grow up to become a great and holy king who would unify the world. This prediction led his father to be afraid that he would give up royal life to become a holy man, so he was careful to protect him from the reality and pain of the world.

But after 29 years of luxury, with servants, cooks, and guards to care for him, Siddhartha grew curious about the real world and asked his father to let him leave the palace. At last his father decided to let him go and explore the world beyond the palace walls.

The Four Sights

During his excursions, Siddhartha saw four "sights" that led him onto the spiritual path. First of all, he saw an old person—evidence that life was always changing, that things could never remain the same. He saw a sick person and was shocked by their pain and suffering. On his next trip, he saw a corpse—undeniable evidence of impermanence. Then finally he saw a spiritual seeker, someone who was looking to move beyond attachment to the physical world and transcend pain and suffering. This seeker had nothing, but seemed to have everything, for he was at peace.

All this made a great impression on Siddhartha. He decided to release himself from all his worldly possessions and go in search of truth. He removed all his gold, surrendered all his worldly possessions, and went searching for the answers to life and a way to help humanity transcend suffering.

Becoming Enlightened

The prince became a wandering man making his way down the river Ganges. He met many holy men along the way, all with different pathways to enlightenment and mastery, and tried anything and everything, but couldn't find the answers he was looking for. One day, he decided to sit under a bodhi tree and not move until he had found those answers. He undertook a deep inner dialogue, retracing all his steps and contemplating his awareness, and then he came up against a demon, Mara, the manifestation of temptation and the epitome of fear. The prince remained unshakable; he placed his hands on the ground and called the Earth to be his witness. As Mara came towards him, he looked deep into the eyes of fear and smiled. Mara vanished and the prince became instantly enlightened.

Master of Ancient Wisdom

The Buddha is one of the Divine Masters of ancient wisdom and one of the enlightened beings residing upon the spiritual plane who is dedicated to the self-mastery and ascension of the human race. He is beyond the need for physical expression and the best way to describe his energy is simply "golden."

When I invite him to appear to me, I am transported deep within myself, into a giant cave. In the center is an Indian man with deep brown skin and long dark hair. Golden light is radiating from his heart. He explains that his purpose is to awaken the same golden energy in all those who connect with him.

Just like the Buddha, we can all have powerful dialogues in which we check in with the divine intelligence that resides within. It's in this space that we will also come into contact with our greatest fears and the most wrathful aspects of our inner doubt system. The Buddha's message is simple: don't run from fear, look it in the eye and smile. When we become scared, we are overwhelmed by *possibility*, not by truth, and by looking in the eye of fear, instead of running away from it, we become one with it. This is enlightened action.

Working with the Buddha

Working with the Buddha can support you with:

© overcoming unhealthy attachments to physical things or people

© distinguishing between the voice of fear and the voice of love

© facing your greatest fear

© becoming more connected to your true self

Master Buddha's activation calls forth the inner teacher, the buddha within. When this wise and resilient aspect of yourself comes to the forefront of your mind, you have a more enlightened view of life and the world.

INNER TEACHER ACTIVATION

Place your hands on your heart space, palms facing down, and breathe toward them. Set the intention to arrive at the inner cave of your heart. Become aware that in the center of that cave is Master Buddha, who is a personification of the great teacher you have within.

Say:

> *Master Buddha, great exalted teacher, one with all, thank you for blessing me with your golden light.*
>
> *I am willing to face every aspect of myself, including my fears and doubts.*
>
> *I recognize that sometimes I am frightened more by possibility than truth.*
>
> *I smile at my fear. I smile at my doubts. I become one with them all.*
>
> *In my heart space, Master Buddha, I welcome your guiding light.*
>
> *Thank you for helping me become one with the teacher I have within, waiting to be called up and out, the part of me that has never left the infinity that is whole.*
>
> *I call the great teacher I have within.*
>
> *Inner buddha, ancient teacher, keeper of wisdom, stand at the forefront of my being today, be guided by Master Buddha.*
>
> *I surrender to your infinite intelligence. I give you permission to lead the way.*
>
> *And so it is.*

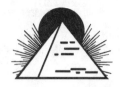

THE DIVINE DIRECTOR

The Divine Director is an advanced cosmic light being from the heart of Source who is dedicated to helping the Earth and all of her inhabitants align with divine purpose. The Director works closely with the archangelic sphere and the guardian angels to ensure that they are fulfilling their duties and helping the humans they are "charged" with protecting.

The Divine Director is one of the more elusive Divine Masters. There's not a lot of information on this being and what there is has never fully resonated with my energy. But it's important to know that as the Divine Director is a cosmic being, they can be beyond our comprehension. They are definitely beyond physical appearance or form, but will create one so that we can have a personal connection with them.

When I connected clairvoyantly to the Divine Director, they appeared in a masculine form with handsome features, deep brown eyes, and deep brown skin, wearing a Space Command uniform. I felt a warmth and a personal resonance and was excited to make the connection.

The best way to imagine the Divine Director would be to think of a managing force of the heavens. This intergalactic spiritual guide is dedicated to helping us understand purpose, live with purpose, and express ourselves in a purposeful way. If you're trying to understand what will bring you closer to feeling purposeful or you're trying to get to the bottom of what your purpose is, the Divine Director can guide you.

Living Purposefully

It's important to acknowledge that purpose is influenced by perception. We all have a different idea about what it means to live purposefully, and of course our perception will absolutely influence how we live. What's amazing about working with the Divine Director is that they will help you understand how you can live purposefully and authentically.

From personal experience, I believe that purpose is about doing what lights us up. If whatever we love doing is respectful to others or even beneficial to others (including the Earth), then we are living purposefully. Being purposeful is about sharing our gifts. Gifts cannot be gifts unless they are shared, so when we begin to share ours, we create a clearer alignment with regard to how we can serve and be served in the world.

It's important to know that purpose goes beyond career, especially as it often seems that purpose and career have become interwoven in modern-day spirituality. They can be connected, but they don't have to be. I like to think that purpose is what lights us up and helps us light up the world. Our career is what we do to make a living. That can support our purpose, and if they fuse together, that's amazing, but never let your soul's purpose be defined by a business card or title.

Understanding Lessons

The Divine Director works directly with the Karmic Board and has access to the Akashic records. These record all the events of all the lifetimes, incarnations, experiences, and journeys of all the incarnated beings ever. Many of us have huge lessons to experience in this lifetime. These lessons aren't all previously orchestrated, but may unfold when we move in a certain direction or follow through on certain decision.

When we experience a challenge or difficulty, we often can't get to the bottom of why it happened or why a chain of challenging events unfolded the way it did. It's important to flag here that Source is always working for our greatest good, and even though some experiences feel like punishments, they're not. It's also important to say that every challenging experience can teach us something, but such experiences aren't orchestrated that way, they just unfold based on circumstances.

With all of that being said, you can call on the Divine Director to shed light on a challenging experience or help you to identify the pattern, belief, or false narrative that may have contributed to that experience. Through prayer and meditation you can ask and receive direct support in getting to the bottom of it. The Divine Director will access the Akashic records and give you a deeper understanding so that you can make the shifts you need to move forward in a more fearless way.

Prayer for Understanding Lessons

Thank you, Divine Director, for helping me understand the lessons connected to this situation.

Thank you for lighting up in my mind the limiting beliefs, patterns, and choices that have led to this unfolding.

I am willing to have a higher perspective on this current situation and all of the circumstances that led to this moment.

I am willing to be led by your light toward a peaceful resolution, so that I can experience the contentment I deserve.

Thank you for leading the way.

And so it is.

Divine Intervention

All of us can reach a point where we need help with a particular issue, situation, or challenge. It's the point where we've tried absolutely everything, and nothing has helped. This is the time for divine intervention.

Divine intervention is when we create energetic and emotional space for spiritual support. It's the moment when we get out of the way and let light lead. It's a powerful moment when a miracle or healing shift occurs.

The Divine Director is a powerful guide who helps us to know that not only are shifts and miracles possible, but we deserve them. In order for them to occur, we just have to step to the side, hand over the situation, and let the Divine Director and their Intergalactic Command lead the way. The Divine Director works directly with angels, guides, the Akashic records, and the light of Source to curate, cooperate, and guide. If you are in a challenging situation and nothing is changing, healing, or unfolding, call in this intergalactic light to lead the way.

Working with the Divine Director

Working with the Divine Director can:

- help you be clearly connected to your spiritual and angelic guides
- enable you to understand lessons, challenges, and the patterns that created them

◎ guide you to get out of your own way and welcome heaven's help

◎ help you have a clearer connection to your life purpose

The energetic activation that the Divine Director offers creates an opportunity for you to be led to deeper purpose and fulfillment in life.

DIVINE INTERVENTION ACTIVATION

Close your eyes.

Breathe deeply.

Bring your focus to your forehead, your third eye center.

Visualize yourself being immersed in purple and indigo light.

Let that light transport you to the etheric realm.

See yourself surrounded by stars. You may even find yourself standing before the Divine Director and their Intergalactic Command.

Say:

> *Divine Director, intergalactic star commander, thank you for stepping into my energy body at this time.*
>
> *I am at a pivotal point in my own personal journey where I am ready to grow, expand my knowledge, and remember the ancient wisdom of my soul.*
>
> *I choose to awaken the ancient wisdom of my soul now.*
>
> *I choose to connect with the ancient wisdom of my soul now.*
>
> *I am ready to be connected and aligned with purpose.*

Thank you for helping me understand the true meaning of purpose.

Thank you for helping me unlock the secret teachings of my incarnations, past and present.

I am ready to be filled by the wisdom of the stars.

I am ready to welcome divine intervention.

I remember that I was born on purpose, for a purpose, and to live with purpose.

I am ready to live purposefully.

I am aligned with your light.

I am guided by galactic supporters.

Thank you for upgrading my frequency accordingly.

Thank you for imparting any messages I need to hear.

I am ready.

And so it is.

Take a moment to breathe.

Become aware of any information, images, signs, or downloads you receive.

Know the Divine Director is leading the way.

Djwal Khul

Djwal Khul (pronounced Dwaahl Cool), also known as "the Tibetan," is a Tibetan Buddhist master who is said to have had many incarnations and to have been one of the original devotees of the Buddha and one of the three wise men who honored the baby Jesus with frankincense, gold, and myrrh. He was one of the original masters, or Mahatmas, presented in the work of Helena Blavatsky, featured in the Mahatma Letters (*see p.15*), sometimes signing off with "DK," and is said to have become a spiritual guide and divine confidant of Alice Bailey.

According to Theosophy, Djwal Khul has esoteric knowledge of an ancient secret path known as "the Ageless Wisdom tradition." He is described as a member of the Great White Brotherhood who has now ascended beyond traditional philosophy and religion and offers a more cosmological understanding of the universe.

Djwal Khul's divine mission is to guide humanity toward a more enlightened and compassionate existence. He is one of the lamas residing in the etheric retreat known as Shambhala (*see p.11*) and is a leader of a large group of lamas who are dedicated to bringing light to the world. Many of these lamas are now spiritual guides to lightworkers.

Every time I connect with the energy of Djwal Khul, I am transported on a telepathic level to a monastery at the top of a high mountain. Instantly I can hear lamas doing deep throat chanting and I can smell spices and incense burning. Prayers are being said and bells being rung in the temple room.

Djwal Khul appears as a Tibetan monk, except his hair has grown out and he is wearing a silky golden robe. He has a beard shaped into a point. His eyes are golden brown. Being in his presence lights me up from the inside out and makes me feel spiritually aligned. I get the impression that through his early experiences in many lifetimes he learnt the importance of discipline, trust, and spiritual practice. Although I don't hear his voice, I seem to receive the message that it's important to trust the path that we are on and to allow it to unfold over time.

Dharma

I've had several encounters with lamas and Tibetan monks on my own spiritual path. For some reason, wherever I go in the world I seem to come across these incredible beings. It feels as if in some way Djwal Khul is orchestrating these meetings. It may be his light working through the monks I have encountered.

One time when I was visiting a friend in New York, we went into an amazing Tibetan and Buddhist store. It was a lovely place selling a lot of Buddhist artifacts and handmade Tibetan treasures. I bought several items, including a photograph of His Holiness the Dalai Lama. The man who owned the store was clearly Tibetan, but seemed to be a householder rather than a monk, as he wore a wedding ring and there were photographs of him with his family on the altar. That night, I had a dream about him. In my dream, he was a monk and I was being blessed or initiated by him. I found it strange. When I told my friend, who's a practicing Buddhist, the next day, she said, "Although not everyone knows, the owner of that store used to be a lama, but he left the monastery because he fell in love with his wife."

That was my first trip to New York and the next day I went exploring. I was looking for a music store, but a series of "wrong turns" led me back to the Tibetan store instead. I peered inside and saw it was empty apart from the owner. So I went in.

"I was here yesterday. You may remember, I bought the…"

"Yes, I remember."

I took a deep breath. "This might seem strange, but I feel that I was supposed to come back today. Last night, I had a dream, and in the dream, you were a lama among other lamas and monks in the Himalayas, and I was being initiated by you. I felt that I should tell you about it."

The man came out from behind the till, pulled down the blinds, and locked the door. Then he led me over to an altar and began to pray in Sanskrit, singing, chanting, and bowing. It was just like my dream, except I was in the center of New York City.

When the man had finished, he tied a red string around my wrist, knotted it several times, and said I should now walk the path of *dharma*, which is Sanskrit for "purpose."

I believe this was orchestrated by Djwal Khul. He is a master of *dharma*. He helps us align to our path so that we can allow it to unfold as it needs to. If you are finding it difficult to understand your path right now, or you want to know how it is going to unfold, working with the energy of Djwal Khul will help you to trust the process.

Working with Djwal Khul

Working with Djwal Khul can help you:

© connect with the Tibetan monks and masters of the Himalayas

© remember past-life information regarding the Buddha

© find a deeper purpose to your life

Djwal Khul's activation is about helping you step onto the ever-unfolding path of *dharma*. This energetic anchor will help you feel more connected to your path and encourage you to trust in its unfolding.

DHARMA ACTIVATION

Take a moment to meditate on your life path. If you have any uncertainty about the unfolding of a particular aspect of it, think of it now.

Take several deep breaths.

When you're ready, welcome DK and his *dharma* activation with this intentional prayer:

> *Djwal Khul, master of ancient wisdom, leader of great lamas and lords of light, thank you for shining your golden light upon me.*
>
> *I welcome your energetic embrace and support in the greater unfolding of my life.*

I surrender to you my fears, concerns, and attachments to my dharma.

Thank you for helping me trust in the greater purpose of my life.

Thank you for helping me tap into the gifts and strengths I hold within so they can help me live with greater quality and meaning.

I welcome your golden rays of sunlight into my heart, my mind, and my body, so that I can light up in ways I have never lit up before.

I step back and allow my path to unfold like a thousand-petaled lotus.

And so it is.

EL MORYA

El Morya, also known simply as Morya, is another of the Masters of Ancient Wisdom introduced to the world through the founder of the Theosophical Society, Helena P. Blavatsky (*see p. 5*). Morya was made popular through the 1,400 pages of "Mahatma Letters" that Madame Blavatsky exchanged with A.P. Sinnet.

The true identity of Morya, or "M," was a mystery, but it was most likely a pseudonym used to protect the identity of Ranbir Singh, a spiritually aware man who was born into a powerful family that ruled Kashmir in the 19th century. It is said that he interceded both spiritually and physically to stop the British invasion of the region in 1845.

There has been much speculation about Morya's connection with Helena Blavatsky. Was he a living master contacting her through the astral realms? Or the spirit of an ascended soul who was contacting her telepathically from the spiritual world? We'll never truly know, but what's interesting is that the Mahatma Letters stopped only one year before Ranbir Singh passed away.

According to the Theosophical Society, El Morya had many incarnations on Earth and was Melchior, the wise man who gave myrrh to the baby Jesus, as well as one of the emperors of Atlantis.

When I energetically call El Morya into my space, this royal presence appears as an Indian man wearing robes and a turban that is embellished with a bright sapphire-blue crystal. He has an aura of bright blue and pure white light. The sound of chanting fills my ears. El Morya's energy feels similar to that of a protective guardian angel. I know he is trustworthy, is aligned to divine truth, and is working for God.

Energy Protection and Boundaries

As, during his last incarnation, El Morya was able to protect Kashmir from invasion by the British, he is one of the souls in the Great White Brotherhood who is able to protect us on a spiritual level and remove from our energy anything that is not serving our life, purpose, and connection with God. He is strongly associated with the Blue Ray, the spiritual energy that helps us be unshakable in our truth and intent.

El Morya helped me understand that many of us try to protect ourselves from vibrations that are conflicting with our own by using our own energy and our own vibration, for example by visualizing ourselves in a bubble, but this can lead to us becoming depleted. In order to be completely safe, we must align with the protection of a higher power, ultimately God. Now I know that if I ask angels and masters for protection, knowing that they are messengers of God, my own energy reserves will be preserved and I will have the ultimate spiritual protection.

El Morya is closely connected to Archangel Michael, the archangel of the Blue Ray. We can call on them together for strength, courage, and the confidence to set boundaries, as well as for the removal of psychic daggers. A psychic dagger can enter our being when someone thinks ill of us, even if they're not meaning to send it. Other people's ill will can often hurt us, destabilize us, and even hold us back.

SCANNING FOR PSYCHIC DAGGERS

Close your eyes.

Imagine your energy field.

Scan it from head to toe.

If your energy appears muted or hazy, then there's a good chance there's something negative there that you've picked up from your day. You may even see some sort of talon, dagger, or arrowhead in a part of your energy body.

Once you've identified where it is, use this prayer:

> *Thank you, El Morya and Archangel Michael, for removing the talons, daggers, limitations, dark thoughts, limiting thoughts, ill intentions, fears, or any other negative thought pattern, idea, or intention from my energy body.*
>
> *I invoke the Blue Ray of Protection and the Golden Ray of Christ Light into my energy field and step into the heart of unconditional love.*
>
> *I surrender the need to fight.*
>
> *I am safe.*

In your mind, visualize the Blue and Golden Rays washing through your being, especially around the part where the dagger has been removed. See this light as an ointment cleansing, healing, and sealing the opening in your energy field.

Awakening Presence

Part of El Morya's mission is to help us in times of challenge on our spiritual journey. He can energetically guide us to know what road to take, to intuit who and what is trustworthy, and to set powerful boundaries when we need to say no. He can help us trust in our own voice, our capacity to have authority, and our innate connection to the Divine.

The I AM Presence (*see p.92*) is ultimately our connection to the Oneness of life. When we connect to it, we remove all energetic blocks and ideas of separateness and step into a space where everything is one. Working with El Morya, we're able to begin forging this direct connection. He encourages us to recognize that we deserve our very own connection with the Divine.

Should you ever find yourself struggling with your spiritual connection, you can call on El Morya and share your concerns, just you would with a good friend.

Working with El Morya

Working with El Morya:

© helps you stand unshakable and firm, especially with boundaries

© helps you establish your own personal relationship with God

© supports you in connecting with the power of the I AM

© can support you in protecting your energy from lower vibrations

This energetic activation allows you to connect with the infinite light of the universe. It is protective and supportive, allowing you to purposefully connect with inspiration and guidance.

I AM ACTIVATION AND INVOCATION

See yourself surrounded by an incredible golden light.

Inhale deeply. Exhale and affirm:

> *I AM the light.*

See all the living beings on the planet connected to one another. See them as one. See them surrounded by golden light.

Inhale deeply. Exhale and affirm:

> *YOU ARE the light.*

See yourself uniting with all the souls in heaven and on Earth.

Inhale deeply. Exhale and affirm:

> *WE ARE the light.*

Pause. See yourself beyond time and space, aligned with your Creator.

Inhale deeply. Exhale and affirm:

> *I AM one with all that is.*
>
> *I AM.*
>
> *I AM.*

El Morya's activation helps you to become aware of the light and presence of God. This is a wonderful intentional prayer to help you go beyond any past limitations, so that instead of having someone else's opinion of the Divine, you have your own direct experience.

AWAKENING PRESENCE ACTIVATION

Visualize your energy field being immersed in a sapphire blue light.

See divine light coming from the heart of Source and penetrating the crown of your head.

Let this clear light fill your being. See the cup of your heart filling with goodness.

El Morya comes to you, meeting you heart to heart.

El Morya recognizes the light of God in you and around you.

Say:

> *Thank you, El Morya, for activating the I AM Presence in me.*
>
> *It feels so good to remember I AM one with all that is.*
>
> *I welcome your guidance and leadership as I recognize that I am worthy of my own personal connection with God.*
>
> *Thank you for guiding me to set healthy boundaries in my life so that I can honor my soul and my own personal needs with more time.*
>
> *I welcome your Blue Ray into my energy at this time, so that I can stand strong and trust in the clarity of my soul's voice and wisdom.*

Thank you for guiding me toward the next phase of my soul's evolution.

I am grateful to know you are here.

I am grateful to be one with God.

And so it is.

GAIA

In Greek, *gaea* is "land" or "earth," and Gaia is a goddess figure who is the physical embodiment of the Earth itself, but more than that, she is the spiritual force or spiritual identity of the Earth. She is the life that moves through the plants, the sweetness in the honey, the air that encourages the bees to fly. Her kiss is on every animal's forehead. She is the being that we can connect with on a spiritual level to develop our very own relationship with the planet that we call home.

Grounding and Earthing

Getting grounded or "Earthed" has been acknowledged as a very powerful healing modality and way to become more connected and aware as a human being. When we walk barefoot on the land, sand, or earth, or even put our feet in the ocean, we give permission for the spirit and presence of Gaia to root us back down to Earth. Through the process of "Earthing," we release all the negative energy, concerns, and extra energies that we are carrying to the Earth. Don't worry about doing this—Gaia and her guardians have the capacity to transform these negative energies back into positive. Just like plants breathing in CO_2 (thank you, Earth Mother), she draws down negative energy from our being, purifies it, and turns it into energy that fuels life.

Queen of the Elementals

Elementals are the angels of the Earth, spiritual beings known in the Celtic tradition as the "fae," who are the overseers and protectors of land and sea. They can work with us and help us to become more connected to our emotions, our body, and ultimately the life-force that runs through us. They have been part of many cultures and described in many different ways. I simply call them "guardians," as I see them as similar to angelic beings, but with a more "rustic" nature (pun intended).

Gaia sends these divine beings on Earth-based missions to help the planet survive and thrive, even while the human race continually disrupts her natural ebb and flow.

There are four groups of guardians, who have many different names. To keep it simple, I break them down by elements:

Earth Guardians

Earth guardians are the divine beings who look after the plants and animals that are connected directly to the Earth. They can help us tap into Earth energy to become more grounded, rooted, and focused in our endeavors.

Air/Wind Guardians

Air or wind guardians are the energetic presences who look after the wind, the air we breathe, and the birds that fly. They can help us tap into the energy of thought and shift our perception so we can breathe more easily.

Fire Guardians

Fire guardians are the divine beings who look after the natural forces of fire that exist in the Earth. They are the guardians who preside over the Earth's mantle, lava, and even volcanoes. They can help us direct our energy and will and express the fire we hold within.

Water Guardians

Water guardians are the divine guardians of waters and seas. They look after all the animals and beings who live in water, and they also help the tides to flow. They can help us tap into our emotions and express how we really feel.

Working with Gaia

Gaia is working with everyone who is doing what they can to protect the Earth. She is a wonderful spiritual guide for conservationists, animal rights activists, and any other eco-activists. She will inspire you, guide you, and help you raise awareness in order to contribute to greater environmental healing.

Working with Gaia can help you:

©   connect with the Earth and become more grounded

©   tap into your natural emotions and human traits

©   become a better partner and guardian of the planet

©   with any sort of Earth-based activism

Gaia's activation is about getting more connected to the planet. In this intentional prayer, you welcome the guardians of the four directions and Great Mother and ask them to anchor you into the Earth.

EARTH CONNECTION ACTIVATION

This activation is best done by placing your feet on the Earth. If you can, go out into the country or to the ocean and place your bare feet onto the land or sand. If you cannot go outside for whatever reason, imagine that your bare feet are on the land.

See deep roots coming from them and going down into the Earth. Feel the Earth Mother pulling you down and anchoring you into her.

Say:

> *Lady Gaia, Great Mother, Planet Earth, thank you for holding me, hosting me, and nourishing me every day.*
>
> *I am so grateful to you.*
>
> *Thank you for drawing my energy down into you and uniting us.*
>
> *It feels so good to know that we can become one in this way, feet to Earth, soul to soul.*
>
> *I AM one with you.*
>
> *Guardians of the four directions, I welcome you into this space.*
>
> *Earth guardians, thank you for rooting me, for helping me access Earthly wisdom.*
>
> *Air guardians, thank you for being the wind beneath my wings and for helping me have a clear awareness of life.*

Fire guardians, thank you for being the warmth in my heart and for showing me how my passions can become my purpose.

Water guardians, thank you for being the life in my blood and for helping me trust that my emotions are great gifts and messengers.

I welcome in Gaia, goddess of the Earth.

Thank you, Great Mother Gaia. I am uniting with you.

I AM rooted.

I AM grounded.

I AM one with the Earth.

And so it is.

If you are outdoors, spend some time connecting with nature. Let Gaia inspire you.

GREEN TARA

Green Tara is one of the most loved and respected female deities in many Buddhist traditions and is well regarded across the world. She is not only celebrated as an enlightened being who can guide us in life, but also revered as a goddess and an aspect of the Divine Feminine.

The goddess Tara is said to appear in many colors, including red, yellow, blue, white, and green. The white and green forms are said to be her most compassionate.

When I connect to Tara, she appears in her green form. It feels to me that this is the most relevant to those of us who want to make a deeper connection to the teacher within and experience the enlightened aspects of our true self. When I call her in, she first appears as a green cloud-like energy, then, as the energy lingers, I see an angelic figure begin to form—an Asian figure with the most incredible clear and bright skin. Her eyes are chestnut brown and the green and golden light of her aura penetrates my soul. I'm awe-struck by her presence, and all my apprehensions, anxieties, and concerns fade away. Green Tara's presence feels like sunlight breaking through clouds, lighting up the world.

Tara is Sanskrit for "star" or "planet," and therefore this Divine Master is linked with navigation and travel, for the ancient wise ones of the Earth navigated by the stars. I feel Tara is an intergalactic presence—she goes far beyond this realm.

Bodhisattva

The story goes that Tara is an aspect or extension of Avalokitesvara, the lord of compassion who, looking at the Earth, cried tears for all those experiencing challenges and pain. His tears became a great river, from which rose a lotus, and from that lotus, Tara was born. It's for this reason that she is associated with compassion and liberation—she was born a being who could come to Earth and bring change. It is also why she is often depicted emerging from a blue lotus flower—it's a symbol of her coming to the Earth to bring light.

In Tibetan Buddhism, there are other forms of grace or compassion that have manifested from the heart of the universe to help us experience our truth and walk our path. They are known as bodhisattvas. They are angel-like beings who embody the highest form of enlightenment and love. In the Mahayana tradition, many practitioners have the goal of becoming a bodhisattva one day, for it is said that when you dedicate your life to liberation and truth, you can become one of these beings of enlightenment. This is very similar to the more recent concepts of ascension and becoming an Ascended Master.

Through my studies, I've come to see bodhisattvas as somewhere between Ascended Masters and angels. Through the work of Robert Thurman, leading professor of Indo-Tibetan studies at Colombia University, I have come to understand that essentially bodhisattvas are the archangelic beings of Tibetan Buddhism. There are many similarities. So to help you understand the true essence of Green Tara, think of her as part angel, part goddess—a being of grace, light, and compassion who can guide you on your path.

Mother of Liberation, Supreme Protectress

Green Tara is dedicated to helping all who call on her reach a state of absolute liberation—liberation from greed, attachment, and anything that's keeping us from connecting to the divine aspects of ourselves. She is an incredible guide, particularly for women or those connecting with their feminine aspects, helping them to overcome oppression and the belittlement of others or even "the system." She can help us detach from the limiting ideas, thoughts, and energies of people, places, situations, and belief systems, or from anything else that is standing between us and greatness. She uses her powerful, graceful light to sever the bonds that are binding us to limiting situations or stories, so that we can be free to step into our most enlightened self.

Green Tara is also a fierce protectress who can wrap us in rainbow light to protect us from lower vibrations, the opinions of others, or any other negative energies that are preventing us from being our true selves. If you are reclaiming parts of yourself that you have ignored, or felt ashamed of, or been discouraged from expressing, Green Tara will detach you from dramas, wrap you in rainbow light, and align you with the energy of liberation.

No Mud, No Lotus

Finally, Green Tara is a universal symbol of hope. All of us will at some point experience the challenge of feeling held back, stuck, and unmotivated. Green Tara will help us understand that the shit in our life can become fertilizer. If you feel stuck in the mud, know that she will help you emerge from it and grow into a beautiful lotus.

Working with Green Tara

Green Tara is a guiding light in the darkness. By calling on her, you can experience:

© divine guidance that will liberate you

© freedom from bonds, stories, and attachments

© the strength to emerge from a muddy situation into the light

© the blossoming of your true self

GREEN TARA'S SANSKRIT CHANT

To align with the guiding starry energies of Green Tara, why not try her Sanskrit chant? Traditionally, this is sung 108 times (a sacred number) as a daily practice to welcome her liberation into your world.

OM Tare, Tu Tare, Ture, Soha
(pronounced: Om Tarey, too tarey, turey swvaah ha)

OM: The sound of Oneness; *Tare*: O Tara; *Tu*: I pray; *Tare*: O Tara; *Ture*: Truthful one; *Soha*: So be it.

Green Tara's activation is a simple devotional prayer that calls you into her heart, where you are held in her compassionate light.

REFUGE ACTIVATION

OM Tare, Tu Tare, Ture, Soha

Green Tara, supreme protectress, mother of liberation, thank you for accepting me into your heart space.

I step into your guiding light of liberation, compassion, and peace.

Thank you for freeing me of all attachments.

Thank you for severing the cords of fear.

I step into your heart space and claim liberation as my truth.

Thank you for guiding me with your light.

I emerge from the mud like a lotus rising up toward the sun.

And so it is.

HATHOR AND THE HATHORS

Hathor, also known as Het-Heru, is the ancient cow goddess of ancient Egypt, a solar goddess who is strongly connected to the sky and fertility. Hathor worship dates back to the third millennium BCE. She is an easily recognized goddess figure, for she wears a sun disk on her head, held in place by two horns (relating to the cow). Another widely known image of her is a human-like being with a pair of cows' ears. She has many faces and icons in the sacred temples of Egypt. Many columns have her cow-eared image around the top.

Het-Heru means "from the house of Horus" and it has become accepted that Hathor is the divine consort of the hawk-headed deity Horus. This connection gives Hathor cosmic energy and a link to the stars, star beings, and star potential. It is also believed that she is most likely the daughter of the sun god, Re, and therefore carries the infinite light of the sun.

Through Egyptian iconography, hieroglyphics, and folklore, we learn that Hathor is "the beautiful one," and she is strongly associated with female power, sexuality, and sensuality. Many people have associated her energy with that of Aphrodite, the Greek goddess of love.

Cosmic Cow Goddess

Throughout the ages, in all parts of the world, the cow has been respected and associated with motherhood, most likely because it is a wonderful producer of milk. As Hathor is a cow goddess, she too becomes inextricably associated with fertility, motherhood, and the producing of milk, which nurtures growth and strength.

Hathor is a wonderful goddess figure to call on if you are wanting to work with your mother's ancestry, get pregnant, or nurture the energy of a project that you'd like to give birth to.

Working with Hathor

Working with Hathor:

© helps you reclaim sexual power

© can support fertility and reproduction

© strengthens your connection to the cosmos

The Hathors

The Hathors are a race of extraterrestrial light beings that are assigned to those working with the light and activation energy upon the Earth. Connecting with the light they bring to the world is like connecting with the light in the heart of the sun. I believe that the many columns across Egypt headed with the cow-face of Hathor refer to the fact that these beings, on an energetic level, appear as columns of incredibly bright light and are dedicated to bringing the brilliant light of many suns to our world. The Hathors themselves exist on a multi-dimensional level and are able to connect to lightworkers in this realm via meditation, telepathy, and divine inspiration.

I was first introduced to the Hathors through the work of Tom Kenyon. I was doing my Reiki Master training in 2011, and my Reiki Master for this training, Roisin, had been on several trainings and retreats with Tom. She gifted me a copy of one of his books, *The Hathor Code*. After reading that book, I decided to delve in and have my own experience of the Hathors if it was available to me, and it led me to where I am today with them.

I believe that Hathor is the goddess/high priestess of this group of light beings and that she incarnated in ancient Egypt and/or was connected to the magical and ancient mystery schools there. When I am connecting with her, she seems to be a single figure, but in fact she represents an entire race of beings who come into the space when you call her in. I love the idea that an entire civilization was headed up by the cosmic sky guardians Hathor and Horus.

The Hathors are dedicated to the evolution of the human soul. They are aligned to the energy of ascension and helping us hold more space for light. When I encounter them, it feels as though I am being teleported to an ancient temple ground where there are many beings gathering in peace. I am completely filled up with the energies of love and light, and it feels as though I am taking a bath in greatness.

Even though they are from a higher dimension than the one that we are in now, the Hathors are in touch with the rest of the Ascended Masters and aligned to the energy of the Divine Director, who assigns spiritual guides and guardians to those incarnated on the Earth (*see p.117*). When we work with them, they help align our vision—they can help us have laser-beam focus and remember why we have felt drawn to developing spiritually in the first place.

As you are someone who is walking the spiritual path and working on the evolution of your soul, working with these beings will be incredible for you. They will replenish you with their presence. If you feel particularly drawn to Hathor, then there is a good chance that one of your guides is Hathorian.

Working with the Hathors

Working with the Hathors:

© supports your spiritual evolution

© helps you welcome more light into your being

© allows you to bathe in pure light to upgrade your energetic frequency

© brings you more guidance on the path ahead

This activation is a spiritual DNA upgrade. Through connecting with the energy of the Hathors, you will be able to hold more space for light. The light will support you in unlocking your own spiritual connections and reveal how you can live more purposefully in the world.

HATHORIAN LIGHT-CODE ACTIVATION

Close your eyes and breathe deeply.

Visualize yourself immersed in bright golden light.

Draw down the energy of the stars by visualizing and feeling that you are one with them.

When you're ready, say this intentional prayer:

> *Hathor, Queen of the Hathors, ancient one,*
>
> *Hathors, intergalactic light-bearers and bringers of Infinite Intelligence, thank you for drawing your light codes into my being.*
>
> *I welcome your energetic upgrades and shifts in my frequency.*
>
> *Thank you for unlocking the light in me.*
>
> *Thank you for showing me where my light has not yet reached.*
>
> *I allow myself to bathe in your starlight now.*
>
> *I welcome your programming into my energy centers, knowing it will bring insight into how I can grow, expand, and evolve.*
>
> *I welcome your energies into my energetic field, knowing they will bring love, support, and guidance.*
>
> *Like a column of light, penetrate my being with your infinite intelligence.*
>
> *Light me up with all that I need to know, connect with, and remember.*
>
> *Thank you for pouring your Hathorian codes into my energetic field. I welcome the upgrade now.*
>
> *And so it is.*

HILARION

Hilarion, also known as Hilarion the Great or Saint Hilarion, is a Divine Master who ascended on his physical death and has been dedicating his energy and light to helping the world experience healing and miracles ever since. He was a master healer in the temples of Atlantis and also had incarnations in ancient Egypt. In another incarnation, he was born to pagan parents in Syria in the fourth century AD. He studied in Alexandria, Egypt, where he was converted to Christianity, and it is said that from that moment he dedicated his life to spiritual pursuits. After hearing about the miracles of Saint Anthony, at the tender age of 15 he went off into the desert for two months. He craved personal space, but the hermitage there was busy, so he decided to go back home. Around this time his parents died, so he gave his worldly possessions to his siblings and those in need and retreated to a cave in the wilderness, seeking divine connection.

Caves and Miracles

Hilarion spent the majority of his life living away from humanity. He most likely retreated from the world because he was a highly sensitive being who was like a sponge picking up the energies, fears, emotions and anything and everything else from those who came close. He experienced ill health and loss in his life, and I believe those earthly challenges pushed him deeper into his spiritual practice and led him to understand the power of light and miracles. Through his disconnection from his body, his overwhelming sensitivity, and the loss of his family, he went deeper into his heart space and formed his own personal relationship with Source. I believe the space he created within allowed him to become an incredible bringer of light to the planet, and this light shone on all who came into his presence.

It is said that those who came to Hilarion's cave experienced miracles and it is documented that he cured a woman who could not conceive a child, several children suffering from fatal illnesses, and a paralyzed charioteer. It is also documented that he was able to successfully expel "demons," but I don't think this was necessarily about performing exorcisms, but about helping people overcome their inner demons and experience mental liberation.

Spiritual Perspective

To understand the teachings of the masters, we simply have to look at what they overcame in life. Hilarion therefore helps all those who are sensitive to the world and struggle to cope with the energies down here. If you've ever felt the need to retreat from the harsh energies of others, Hilarion can become a powerful spiritual guide to you, helping you set boundaries and protect your energy field in a way that still allows you to reveal your incredible gifts to the world.

Also, if you have challenging limiting thoughts, Hilarion can help you find the strength to overcome them. In olden times, mental and emotional health challenges were called "demons," as there was no other way to understand them, but in today's world, they can become the true opportunities for us to connect with our emotions, become clearer about what we need, and align our lives to our own growth and healing.

The Emerald Ray

Hilarion appears as a man from Syria or Palestine. He has a bright aura with geometric symbols swirling around it, and his eyes are bright too. They are a blue-gray color, which makes them really stand out. He wears an emerald cloak and his presence feels warm, comforting, and fatherly. It reminds me of Archangel Raphael. I feel they are working from the same energetic healing space.

In modern-day spirituality, Hilarion is regarded as the gatekeeper of the Emerald Ray of Healing. This comes directly from the heart of Source and is dedicated to bringing healing change to the world through science, energetic work, and connection. When we invoke Hilarion, we also welcome in the frequency of the Emerald Ray, which helps initiate the healing changes we need in order to grow, feel more connected to ourselves, and ultimately step into service.

Hilarion is a keeper of ancient healing sciences who can help us understand energy, healing, and connection on a deeper level. He is an amazing Ascended Master for anyone who's working in the sciences, medical, or healing spheres. He will bring you a deeper awareness and understanding of your subject and guide you to fulfill your calling with purpose and passion.

Working with Hilarion

Working with Hilarion can help you:

© experience and express healing energy

© overcome the limitations of sensitivity

© create boundaries that honor your needs

© understand new information that can bring healing change to the world

The Emerald Ray activation brings a deeper understanding of life and light.

EMERALD RAY ACTIVATION

Imagine yourself immersed in emerald light. Imagine yourself stepping into a magical emerald cloak.

Breathe deeply. When you're ready, welcome Hilarion with the words:

Hilarion, master healer, ancient wisdom-keeper,

Thank you for initiating me into the sacred healing sciences. I am willing to have a deeper understanding of life and light.

Thank you for helping me recognize that my sensitivities are gifts and that my emotions are powerful messages from my soul to my body.

I welcome you now. Thank you for immersing my entire being in healing emerald light.

I AM immersed in healing emerald light.

Thank you, Hilarion, for upgrading my frequency so I can unlock the sacred light codes of ancient civilizations and awaken the sacred healer within.

I now tune my frequency and being into the ancient healing arts. I am willing to remember all of the healing arts that are stored in my soul's memory.

I am willing to remember.

I welcome now, into the heart of my being, the blessings, codes, and energetic upgrades of the Emerald Ray.

I am blessed by the Emerald Ray of Source.

I am ignited by the Emerald Ray of Source.

I am initiated by the Emerald Ray of Source.

I am one with the Emerald Ray of Source.

Thank you, Master Hilarion, for this ancient soul awakening.

And so it is.

Bring your hands to your heart space and breathe until you feel you have received the downloads.

HORUS

Horus is one of the earliest, most respected and honored of the Egyptian deities. He is famous for his hawk head and is known as the lord of the sky. The Egyptian word *Her* or *Heru*, from which his name is derived, means "high one," indicating that this deity is a cosmic sky god.

Horus's image is said to illustrate his connection to the sun, moon, and stars: his right eye represents the sun, his left eye the moon, the feathers on his breast the stars, and his wings the sky. He is venerated as the keeper of the cosmos.

Eye of Horus

The Eye of Horus has been adopted the world over as a symbol of protection and guidance. Many people have tattoos, necklaces and even stickers of it, even if they're not connected to the ancient Egyptian mysteries. Horus himself is a highly protective and guiding force, and by working with, meditating on, or even just carrying his Eye symbol, we are invoking his cosmic protection.

Horus is a powerful deity for anyone looking to develop their clairvoyance or spiritual vision. By welcoming his energy into our world, we allow him to unlock, unclog and activate the psychic eyes within us so that we can see the world from a clearer, more resilient space.

Horus has always felt like a very approachable deity to me. He has become one of the masters who have really helped me remember and connect with the more cosmic aspects of my being. It feels as if he has activated the dormant aspects of my starry nature. When I call him in, he arrives through a stargate. I see him standing in front of swirling energy that looks like a giant portal. His skin is almost as black as the midnight sky and his falcon head looks like armor covering his arms and breastbone. Even though his image might seem overwhelming, I feel a clarity and openness in his presence. He is surrounded by starlight and other beings of light representing the star nations he governs.

Keeper of the Cosmic Gateway

Horus is the keeper of the cosmic gateway, an energetic portal through which we can reach hidden realms. This energetic retreat space helps us reclaim the lost ancient wisdom of our soul. When we work with it, we also awaken all the memories and wisdom that allow us to connect with the infinite possibilities of the universe and the power of the stars.

Horus also helps us draw down the power of the stars through the Stellar Gateway chakra (*see p.91*), move beyond time and space, and connect with the infinite wisdom of Source.

Son of Isis

Horus is the son of the goddess Isis. He has a deep and powerful bond with his mother and has often been depicted as an infant suckling her breast. This image, which was recreated for Christianity with Mother Mary and Christ, is a universal symbol of the unbreakable bond between mother and child.

As the son of a goddess, Horus is a wonderful being who honors mothers and will do everything in his power to protect them and their children. It feels to me that he is particularly drawn to single mothers, single-parent households, and mothers who have powerful/hyper-driven sons (I guess that's where my natural connection with him comes from).

Working with Horus

Horus helps with:

© remembering your starry origins

© opening your psychic vision

© mother and child relationships (especially with single parents)

© connecting to the Stellar Gateway chakra and the stars

This activation supports the activation of your Stellar Gateway, allowing you to tap into the totality of possibility. If there is something you are working on manifesting or creating, with this intentional prayer you will connect with the infinite power and potential of the stars, which are ultimately within.

Cosmic Gateway Activation

Breathe deeply.

As you inhale, feel yourself climbing high into the midnight sky.

As you exhale, allow yourself to become one with the energy of the sun, moon, and stars.

Then say this activating prayer:

> *Horus, cosmic sky guardian, keeper of the cosmic gateway, son of Isis, thank you for coming to me now.*
>
> *By the power of sky and stars, by the light of moon and sun, thank you for blessing my energy with your presence.*
>
> *I am willing to activate my inner vision.*
>
> *I am willing to see through your cosmic eyes.*
>
> *I align with the power of infinite space.*
>
> *I align with stellar beings and guides across many moons, many stars, and many suns.*
>
> *I reclaim my star power.*
>
> *I awaken my star power.*
>
> *I step now into the cosmic gateway, empowered, supported, and guided by your light.*
>
> *Horus, O Horus, thank you for blessing me with your cosmic spirit.*
>
> *And so it is!*

ISHTAR

Ishtar is the east Semitic, Akkadian, Assyrian and Babylonian goddess of love and war. She was known as Inanna by the Sumerians and Astarte by the north Semitic peoples. She has had many names and many faces. As long ago as 4000BCE she was acknowledged as queen of heaven, protector of the cosmos, and instigator of truth. She was often depicted with six- and eight-pointed stars, which were originally general symbols of the heavens, but in the Old Babylonian Period, *c.*2000–1600BCE, she became strongly associated with Venus, the planet of love and desire. Many temples were erected to her, and she was invoked and honored in times of war.

Ishtar's name means something like "the desirable" or "the precious," and many have been challenged by the fact that she is linked to both love and war. From my own impressions of the energy she represents, I believe she helps us connect to the root energy of desire, including the desire to fight for what we believe in.

There are many ancient images of Ishtar. Whenever I see one, I see strong connections to the Egyptian goddess Isis (*see p.164*) and also to an angel. When I first tuned in to her, I was pleasantly surprised by her presence. Strong perfume filled the air around me, smelling like amber. Then I was whisked into a hidden temple below the Earth. Before me stood a tall figure, her skin deep mahogany, her features a mix of Asian and African, her eyes made of fire, her whole being bursting with infinite light.

I remember seeing energy swirling all around her. Beings were gathering like armies to her left and right—otherworldly beings with wings, radiating golden and bronze light. They had an angelic energy, reminding me of Archangel Michael and his legion.

When I asked to experience more and understand more about Ishtar's energy, in my mind I saw myself as the rope in a game of tug of war, being pulled in two different directions, and I heard the words "The war between head and heart." It came to me that Ishtar wasn't a goddess of outer war, but of the internal battle we all face when it comes to knowing whether to listen to our head or our heart. Then I heard these rhythmic words being chanted:

I am a guardian, I am the light.
I will guide you through darkness.
I will guide you through the night.

It felt ritualistic, like an initiation of sorts.

It can be challenging for us to figure out if we should listen to our head or our heart. We often find ourselves trying to figure out what each is saying. It seems that Ishtar is the guiding force that helps us through this process.

It also seems that there is something sensual about her, something beautiful that we need to embrace. We humans are sensual beings, sexual beings. Tapping into our sensual and sexual self is in fact spiritual. Through a deeper embrace of our sexual self, we will access a wealth of power stored in the heart of our being.

Working with Ishtar helps us track down the truth of our heart and encourages us to follow it—to follow our passion. It feels as if she's aligned with the integral energy that helps us follow our desires in an authentic way. In ancient times, she was also considered a goddess who could help with all matters regarding fertility and birth. In an energetic sense, this can represent not only conceiving a child but also new projects.

Leader of the Annunaki

Ishtar is the leader of the Annunaki, a race of cosmic light beings that have been coming to Earth, in different forms, from ancient times. The Sumerians acknowledged them as the deities who governed the space between the worlds. When I had my vision of Ishtar, the legions of beings on either side of her were the Annunaki.

Since then, when connecting with Ishtar I have come to see that the Annunaki are similar to the Hathorian race (*see p.146*): an intergalactic force of beings dedicated to helping us rise above darkness. They place codes of bright light into our energy body, so that we can embrace our humanity and ultimately experience the union of body and soul in perfect harmony and trust.

In the distant past, the Annunaki went to the Atlantean civilization and helped those who were aligned with the spiritual path to ascend to the next dimension, so that they could leave the wheel of karma. They were the judges who had to decide who could ascend and who had to be left behind. Those who had not honored the Divine, who had abused their powers, and had not valued the great gift of life that they had been given had to remain behind. For that reason, some people who have had Atlantean incarnations may fear the Annunaki, but I can assure you that they are beings of light.

Working with Ishtar

Working with Ishtar can help you:

©   face and win an inner war

©   distinguish between head and heart

©   conceive a child or other new creation

©   connect with the Annunaki

Ishtar's activation draws in the healing light codes of the Annunaki, so that you can embrace and embody every aspect of your human self in order to align with your highest spiritual form.

ANNUNAKI LIGHT-CODE ACTIVATION

Take a moment. Breathe.

If there's an aspect of your human self you've felt detached from, think of it now. If you have abandoned any aspects of your sensuality or sexuality, set the intention to reclaim them today.

If there's a part of your life that you feel has been draining you or pulling you in two directions, think of it now. Be prepared to know your truth.

Then say:

> *Ishtar, guardian of the heavens, cosmic goddess, maiden, mother, crone, thank you for blessing me with your presence and infinite light.*

Thank you for helping me embrace the aspects of myself I have felt scared or ashamed of.

I call back and reclaim all the parts of my being I have abandoned or rejected.

I rise beyond struggle, I rise beyond constraint.

Thank you, divine goddess Ishtar, for lifting me up and blessing me with your heavenly light.

Annunaki, Annunaki, Annunaki,

I welcome in the presence of the Annunaki people.

Thank you, angelic cosmic beings, for immersing my energy body in your light codes.

Thank you for retuning and realigning my frequency so that I can express the highest, truest, and most complete version of myself.

I welcome your light. Let it penetrate my being, rejuvenate my energy, and upgrade my DNA.

I am replenished.

I am regenerated.

I am reborn.

I am reactivated by Annunaki light.

And so it is.

Bring your hands to your heart space and breathe into it for as long as you need. Don't be concerned if you have any energetic or emotional release. It's a sign that you are aligning to the new frequency.

Isis

Isis is one of the foremost goddesses of the ancient Egyptian pantheon. She is a high priestess, goddess, and mother figure all in one and is strongly associated with the energies of the moon, magic, love, and conquering the underworld.

Isis is the daughter of the Earth god, Geb, and the sky goddess, Nut, therefore she carries the energy of both Earth and sky. Legend has it that she married Osiris, god of the underworld, supposedly her brother, but it's important to remember that these stories are ancient and sometimes hard to fathom with our modern, modest, Western minds. I believe the reason for this marriage would have been to keep the family lineage strong by pairing magical souls together.

Isis is a powerful energy. Through her life experiences, connections, and understanding of magical forces, when it came to her passing, she ascended to master status.

Between Life and Death

In the Pyramid Texts Isis is described as assisting the deceased, and as the wife of Osiris, god of the underworld, she is seen as someone who has overcome the energy of death. Similar to the Death card in the Tarot, this means she can help us be reborn after a challenging situation or a difficult transition. If you ever find yourself in a dark space where the old is dying off around you, Isis will help you transcend fear and despair and re-emerge into the light.

I have always had a strong connection to Isis and Egyptian magic. One time when I was at a yoga nidra class (resting/sleeping yoga), during the extended relaxation we were guided into a transcendental space and encouraged to go deeper and deeper. I remember falling asleep, but becoming fully aware during my sleep state—fully lucid. I remember hearing the voices of my guides and feeling them with me. For some reason, I knew that I would be able to go on a journey, and out of nowhere I said, "Take me to Isis."

Instantly a stargate opened and I went through a wormhole of light and stars. I shot out into the Egyptian desert and flew across it into the center of a giant pyramid. There, standing on an altar, was the goddess herself. She had deep brown skin and she was wearing a headdress of bronze, silver, and gold. She was minimally clothed, with her breasts exposed, but was wearing a huge crystal amulet. She had her arms in a cactus-style position, elbows bent and palms slightly cupped. Energy was shining down upon her from a light somewhere above. I felt instantly humbled and took the knee. I remember feeling I had been initiated into some ancient magical practice, and then in the blink of an eye, I went back the way I had come, landing in my body with a jolt. It was an astonishing experience.

Magic and Priesthood

Isis is a keeper of magical energy; she is dedicated to helping those who feel called to connect with their inner priestess. She helps us see that magic isn't something that comes to us, but an energy we awaken within. She is particularly drawn to those stepping into and honoring their feminine energy.

Through connecting with Isis, we can access the power of the moon and initiate the priestess inside us. Isis will help us claim our power to know, to heal, and to become that strong, powerful and disciplined soul we want to be. It is important to be aware that as she is a goddess who works with the underworld, she will show us aspects of ourselves that need to be faced, reclaimed, and healed. Everything in the shadows will be brought to the light so that we can become a greater vessel for healing light and magic.

Winged Isis and Moon Goddess

There are many images of Isis with wings, reminding us of her cosmic connections. She has the capacity to help us connect with the powers of the heavens and bring them into our heart here on Earth. She can help us access the energies of the stars. She also governs and works with many light beings who are dedicated to helping us spread our wings and fly high.

The moon is strongly associated with Isis, and just as the moon has many phases and aspects, Isis has appeared in Egyptian mythology in many shapes, sizes, and forms. Her magical connection to moon power also represents the cyclic nature of the feminine, which moves through ebb and flow, rather than in a linear fashion. This means that by working with Isis, we can move with the flow of our being and our body's needs.

Working with Isis

Isis can help you with:

© facing the shadow

© claiming your inner magic

© connecting to the power of the moon and stars

- moving through a challenging situation

- honoring the power of the feminine

RECLAIMING MAGIC ACTIVATION

Closing your eyes, take a deep breath.

With each and every inhale, feel yourself reaching upward.

See yourself aligned with the midnight sky. Surrounded by stars. Breathing. Connected. One.

Welcome in Isis with the words:

> *Holy Isis, cosmic light goddess, mother of many, with many names, faces, and forms, thank you for wrapping me in your wings at this time.*
>
> *O mother of magic, moon worker, take me to your inner temples and light the spark of magic in me. I am willing to remember and reclaim the parts of myself that I have cast out, left behind, or been discouraged from developing.*
>
> *I remember and reclaim the lost parts of myself. I call them back from the shadows.*
>
> *I reclaim my most magical aspects.*
>
> *Thank you, Isis, for pouring your lunar light over me now. Thank you for bathing my heart, mind, and energy field in your healing rays as I reclaim my magic.*
>
> *I bow before you and welcome your blessings.*
>
> *I am so grateful to be guided by your presence.*
>
> *And so it is.*

Jesus

Jesus of Nazareth is a bringer of truth. He is a light to the entire universe and a living/dying/spiritual demonstration that forgiveness is possible. When he walked the Earth, he was persecuted for his beliefs and teachings, yet he still loved his human brothers and sisters.

A Multi-dimensional Presence

Jesus is everywhere at once. He is with us right now. He waits for our call and, with the help of his holy angels, he can restore us to our natural light-filled selves. When we call on him, he will bring light to our mind. His presence removes all the blindfolds that prevent us from seeing and all the blockages that stand between us and the miracle we are seeking. He is the voice of love that echoes in our heart, waiting for us to accept that we are forgiven. He helps us to see the light in others, so we can live a life that's filled with miracles and free from condemnation.

Our Brother

Jesus may be a spiritual teacher, but he loves to be recognized as a friend and a brother. He comes to us as an equal and he doesn't ask us to idolize him, but to see that what he has, we have too. He helps us to see that forgiveness is the only choice of our soul. He helps us to eradicate the voice of fear.

Our light is never lost, it is always present, but with life's challenges, it is very easily forgotten and hidden. When we think of Jesus, he will come like a blazing torch into our holy temple, lighting it up. His presence alone banishes all darkness, so we can welcome the acceptance and forgiveness of God.

The Christos/Christ Light

The Christos is an energy of pure unconditional love and acceptance that can only be described as light. Jesus was a vehicle for this light in his human life, as were many spiritual teachers in times gone by, including the Buddha (*see p.113*). This light is available to all of humanity—we all have the capacity to embody it. When Jesus said, "The Kingdom of Heaven is in you," he was talking about the Christ light.

When we call forth that light from the center of our being and ask it to lead us, we begin to see the world through the eyes of Christ and shift into a more forgiving and accepting way of being. This is the pathway of ascension.

Working with Jesus

Call on Jesus to help you with:

© healing

© forgiving those who have hurt you, either emotionally or physically

© accepting that God's only plan for you is love

Jesus's activation draws into your being the light of Christ, that ever-present undying love that will lead you away from all uncertainty and toward a deep inner peace.

CHRIST LIGHT ACTIVATION

Master Jesus, brother of light, vehicle of light, thank you for standing at the forefront of my mind and helping me see the truth.

Like a blazing torch, your light extends to the four corners of my being, removing all darkness and doubt.

In your presence, I welcome your unconditional acceptance and love, as I realize that forgiveness is a natural part of who I am, because it is remembering that as a being of light I can never really be hurt.

I am safe, Jesus, and I know that you are my loving guide.

I welcome you pointing out any areas of my being and my life that require my forgiveness.

With your support, I make the miraculous choice to forgive and be forgiven.

I AM one with the light of Christ.

I AM activated by the light of Christ.

I rest in the light of Christ.

I AM the light of Christ.

Thank you, my friend and brother. And so it is!

JOAN OF ARC

Joan of Arc (Jeanne d'Arc in French), also known as the Maid of Orléans, is a Roman Catholic saint and French heroine widely loved and respected for her role during the Siege of Orléans in the 15th century, during the Hundred Years War, when she was a warrior helping to push the English out of France.

The story goes that Joan was born to parents who owned 50 acres of farmland and her father also worked as a village official. Though they lived in a remote area, the family had connections to the French Crown.

Joan is reported to have been a visionary who encountered Archangel Michael and other saints from the age of 13 onward. Through these encounters, she developed the strength and courage that led her, at the age of 17, to experience the voice of God telling her to expel the English from France. Through her family connections, she was able to organize a meeting with Charles VII of France, in which she related her visions and experiences and he gave her permission to lead the French army into battle.

It is said when the king first met the peasant girl, he wanted to test her spiritual abilities, so he disguised himself as one of his courtiers. When Joan was welcomed into the chamber, she instantly identified him, bowed at his feet, and prayed that God would bless him.

Joan's vision and guidance were accurate. Although she faced some challenges along the way, including resistance from the commanders of the French army, she was able to defeat the English at Orléans.

She was a clearly mystical and well-connected young woman and I genuinely don't think the world was ready for her level of courage and connection. Those in power just couldn't handle the fact that a young woman, wearing what they classed as "men's clothing," was not only a visionary, but a great warrior too. At just 19, Joan was captured and put on trial by the Brits, and was burnt at the stake (twice).

Ascended Master of Truth

Joan of Arc's life was short, but her spirit powerful—her light lives on in the Ascended Master realm and she is ready to support anyone who needs her guidance and courage. One of the greatest life challenges that she overcame was speaking her truth. Her visions could have been put down to "heresy" or "sorcery," but she stuck by her divine guidance and was able to prove that the messages she received were in fact coming from heaven.

If you want to share your truth, whatever that is, Joan of Arc is a Divine Master who will be there to support you through this vulnerable time. Truth is a powerful teacher and authenticity is a quality of spirit. When we align with truth, integrity, and authenticity, we create an openness in our energy field that welcomes in strength and abundance.

It's important to say that truth is different for everyone. For some people, exposing their truest, most authentic self to public gaze isn't safe. Joan knows how this feels. Among other things, she was charged with "cross-dressing." She just couldn't achieve her aims in the way she wanted in the society she was in. If you are finding it difficult to live your truth safely in your current circumstances, Joan will be a sympathetic guide.

Every time I tune in to Joan of Arc's energy I hear the very simple message: "Let truth be your teacher. Let your truth lead the way." It's important to know that sharing and living your truth, with all the openness and vulnerability that entails, is a process. But the more you see and welcome your truth, and are your true self without apology, the more the world is able to see and welcome that truth too.

Overcoming the Fear of Persecution

I've come to understand that the Ascended Masters hold the lessons of all their challenges in their heart so that we don't have to. If we are afraid of something they've experienced or overcome, we can call on them to help us rise above it.

As Joan of Arc was burnt at the stake, she's a master who is able to help us rise above the fear of persecution. Persecution energy is challenging. Maybe you've experienced loved ones criticizing you, or you've felt scared about sharing a deeper aspect of yourself with others or in public, because you've been worried about being judged or misunderstood. Many of those walking the spiritual path fear persecution, and for good reason. If you're scared of sharing your full spiritual self with the world, there's a good chance in a previous incarnation you were persecuted for your beliefs or practices.

Calling in Joan of Arc will overcome this energy of fear. When she reached the Ascended Master realm after being burnt at the stake, she vowed to dedicate her spiritual energy to helping those walking their authentic spiritual path overcome the energy of persecution.

Working with Joan of Arc

Joan of Arc can help you with:

◎ encouraging teenage girls to trust in their abilities

◎ creating a stronger bond with Archangel Michael

◎ speaking your truth and sharing your authentic self

◎ overcoming the fear of persecution or punishment

If you're ready to overcome those fears, call Joan of Arc into your energy now, with the prayer:

Thank you, Joan of Arc, for drawing near and showing me how to overcome the fear of being judged, persecuted, or misunderstood.

Thank you for helping me to have greater trust in myself, my inner vision, and the gifts I was born to bring to this world.

I welcome your guidance and leadership now.

And so it is.

Joan of Arc carries a sword of truth that clears the road ahead. This activation brings clarity and safety.

SWORD OF TRUTH ACTIVATION

Close your eyes.

Visualize yourself immersed in blue light.

Allow the light to create energetic armor around you.

Then say:

> *I invoke the spiritual light of Joan of Arc.*
>
> *Thank you, Joan, for blessing my energy with your presence.*
>
> *I welcome your support, guidance, and encouragement as I step into my most authentic self.*
>
> *It feels so good to know that even though I may feel vulnerable, I am protected by your shield of light.*
>
> *Thank you for placing your sword of power before me and for guiding it to clear my path.*
>
> *I am ready to walk the path of light.*
>
> *I am ready to walk the path of truth.*
>
> *I am ready to move beyond all limiting stories, experiences, and fears.*
>
> *I am aligned with the path of light.*
>
> *I am aligned with the highest truth.*
>
> *The greatest gift I can bring to the world is my whole self.*
>
> *I bring my whole self to the light.*
>
> *I am led by grace.*
>
> *Thank you, Joan of Arc, for giving me the courage you drew on to win your own personal battles and to share your spiritual connection with the world.*
>
> *I am honored to be led by you.*
>
> *And so it is.*

Kali-Ma

Kali-Ma is the Hindu goddess of death and rebirth. She is the destroyer of all evil forces and a protector of liberation (*moksha*). In the Hindu pantheon, she is the most powerful expression of Shakti, which ultimately is an expression of life-force energy in a dynamic feminine form.

In Sanskrit, '*Kala* means "blackness," in reference to the dark night sky, and *Mā* means to "to bring or create," so Kali-Ma is the bringer or creator of darkness. This is not something to fear. Over the years, especially in Western culture, we've been told that "darkness" is bad, when in fact it's a part of life. Before we were born, we were all wrapped in the darkness of the womb, the Earth herself was born in the darkness of the cosmic sky, and every night when we go to sleep, we step back into this space. So the great goddess Kali, the bringer of darkness, is associated with birth, creation, and ultimately renewal. "Bringer of darkness" means the "bringer of greatness."

With that being said, many Hindu and yogic devotees are reluctant to connect with Kali-Ma's energy, and I can understand why. Kali-Ma is a fierce form of divine energy who demands the truth. In her presence, all that is fake, deceptive, or unaligned with integrity will be brought to the surface. She will make us face our greatest fears—not to make us cower, but to help us step into a space of fearlessness. But not everyone is ready to experience the liberation of fearlessness, or own their ultimate truth.

When I've connected with Kali-Ma's energy, it has always been powerful and fiery, but I've never felt scared. In fact, whenever I've come close to experiencing her energy, I've known that great change has been underway, and it's been useful to know that. The best way for me to describe her energy to you would be to ask you to imagine a loving mother, in her most wrathful form, protecting her child from bullies in the playground. You know when a five-foot-nothing woman starts bellowing and roaring because she has seen someone tormenting her child? That's what Kali-Ma's energy is all about.

So, yes, Kali-Ma is strong, fierce, fiery, powerful, and even intimidating, but she is completely loving and will protect all those who call on her. She has dark energy and dark features like the midnight sky, but she's beautiful. When I see her, I see a face made up of starlight. She has darkness all around her, but is illuminated by the light of the cosmos. She is all-consuming and radiant.

Connecting with Fierceness

We live in a world that desires more truth and more integrity. When we get that, we will experience freedom. If you are feeling the need to bust through the blockages that are in your way, preventing you from expressing who you really are, call on Kali-Ma. Like a fiercely protective mother, she will help you get to grips with the truths that you need to know and to own in order to move forward.

A great way to connect with Kali-Ma's energy is to erect an altar in your home and place on it an image of her in her most wrathful form. Go here regularly, keep the space clean, light candles, and connect with her essence.

Working with Kali-Ma

Working with Kali-Ma can help with:

© overcoming fear of the unknown

© learning to trust in darkness

© experiencing a rebirth

© expressing the power you have within

Kali-Ma's activation is about embracing the unknown—she takes you into the darkness and encourages you to step into the fiercest, and most connected form of yourself. This activation calls truth up and out, helping you experience authenticity in order to experience liberation. Do not fear the darkness—it is the energy of cosmic creation.

FEARLESS ACTIVATION

For the best results, do this activation in a darkened room. You may want to have an image of Kali-Ma nearby and a candle to light the way through the process.

With the lights out, apart from a single candle if you wish, drop down into deep breathing and meditation. Think about any aspects of your life that you feel deserve to experience more truth and integrity. Think of aspects of your world where you are willing to surrender to the unknown. What are you holding on to or reaching out for that could be holding you back from liberation?

Bring all of this to your awareness. Then, when you have emerged from this awareness, say this activation prayer:

> *Great mother, bringer of darkness, Kali-Ma, embrace me with your cosmic presence.*
>
> *Guide me to liberation.*
>
> *I was born in darkness. I came from the stars, from the heart of the midnight sky.*
>
> *I am reborn in darkness, embraced by the night and by the light of your love.*
>
> *Where I have held on, I am ready to let go.*
>
> *Where I have held back, I am ready to step forward.*
>
> *Where I have been afraid, I am ready to experience fearlessness.*
>
> *Enter now, great Kali-Ma, into my being.*
>
> *Bless me with your infinite light.*
>
> *Lead me from fear of the unknown into trust in life itself.*
>
> *I am ready to be reborn. I am ready to emerge from darkness and become the light of who I am once more.*
>
> Jai *(praise)*, jai, *Kali-Ma,*
>
> *I am embraced by your love.*
>
> *And so it is.*

KUTHUMI

Master Kuthumi, or Koot Hoomi, known as KH, was one of the original Ascended Masters of Theosophy. He was introduced to the world through the Mahatma Letters (*see p.15*).

There has been much speculation about his true identity, most likely because there's no evidence that such a person actually existed on Earth, and it has become widely accepted that Kuthumi is a pseudonym. According to a lot of researchers, it is likely that he was Sardar Thakur Singh Sandhawalia, a highly intellectual and spiritually committed Sikh who was partially responsible for the campaign that helped Maharaja Duleep Singh to the throne of the Punjab region and who encouraged the Maharaja to reclaim his spiritual path. Helena P. Blavatsky met him during her extensive travels and it is claimed that she reconnected with his soul after he passed to the spiritual realms in 1887.

Evolved Soul

When I connect with the energy of Kuthumi, I feel the presence of a highly evolved soul. He is one of the leaders of the Great White Brotherhood. He has a bright golden aura and is the keeper of the Gold Ray of Ancient Wisdom. He appears as an Indian man. His skin is light brown, his eyes dark brown. He wears a high-collared kaftan shirt and an intricately beaded hat that's similar to a beret. His energy is modest, honorable, and strong.

Since his last physical life was dedicated to spiritual service and many of his other incarnations contributed to healing change upon the Earth, Kuthumi's mission from spirit is to help all souls align authentically with their spiritual path. He encourages us to make a devotional connection to Source in order to have a more sustained spiritual experience.

A Spiritual Doorkeeper

All mediums and channelers need to work with a spiritual "doorkeeper." These beings are angelic bouncers who hold the space for those moving into a transcendental state. This is less about keeping negative energies out and more about looking after people, because we are in a heightened state of vulnerability when we open our heart up in this way.

Kuthumi acts as a spiritual doorkeeper for all who call on him. If you are developing your intuitive and spiritual senses to channel healing or pass on messages from the spiritual realm, or if you are ready to explore more of that realm, you can ask him to wrap you in his golden light of protection. He is a wonderful spiritual guide for anyone who is doing energy work, diving deep spiritually, or seeking to create their own approach to spirituality.

Golden Ray of Ancient Wisdom

The Golden Ray is a spiritual energy that we can call down from Source to access deep wisdom. When we connect with it, we awaken all of the wisdom that we have gained from our past incarnations and also the information that has come directly from the heart of creation and is stored within our energy body. Even just affirming "I am willing to awaken and remember the ancient wisdom within!" on a regular basis will allow us to begin unlocking all of the ancient memories and information we hold.

Another way to welcome in the energy of ancient wisdom is by drawing the Golden Ray into our third eye center, or Ajna. This is the energy center of our spiritual sight and also how we see the world. If we can't see our way forward because we feel blocked, misaligned, or challenged by circumstances, awakening the Ajna with the Golden Ray will allow us to see things differently. Ultimately, awakening the golden Ajna is about being able to see the world through the eyes of an enlightened master (*see the activation below*).

Kuthumi helps us awaken ancient wisdom so that we can have a more sustainable, heightened, and aligned spiritual vision. He knows what it is like to be a human being walking the spiritual path and facing all of the challenges that come with that. If we're trying to align our earthly existence with our spiritual beliefs, Kuthumi will help us do this in a way that feels authentic and supportive of our spiritual expansion.

Visiting Shambhala

Kuthumi is also one of the masters who can help us experience the etheric retreat Shambhala, the spiritual kingdom that contains the wisdom of many elder beings, ancestral spiritual beings, light beings and masters, and the enlightened perspective of the high lamas of the East. Although this is in the Himalayas, it's operating on a higher vibration. We can ask to be taken there in dreams and meditation and also to download spiritual upgrades directly from it.

Once during a sound healing training, I went to do a practice with one of my alchemy crystal singing bowls. The alchemy of this bowl included Tibetan copper and when I was playing it with my eyes closed, I was instantly transported to the top of a snowy mountain. Even though I was there for less than five minutes, I had a strong vision of being wrapped up in blankets and seeing congregations of monks and lamas doing overtone chanting, making a deep-throated vibrational sound. I felt the energy coming into my being and then I started to make the sound with my own voice—a toning sound was coming from my throat with high-pitched "whistles" over the top. When it was over, I found myself lying on my lounge carpet, asking myself, "What just happened?" Later that day I reflected on it in meditation and heard that I had been taken to Shambhala to receive a sound initiation. It was an unforgettable experience.

Working with Kuthumi

Working with Kuthumi can help you:

© deepen your spiritual connection

© dial into the energy of devotion

© align with ancient soul wisdom

© feel safe when exploring deeper spiritual experiences

This activation draws Golden Ray energy into your third eye center to awaken the ancient wisdom within and allow you to have a more heightened and enlightened view of the world and your spiritual path.

ANCIENT WISDOM ACTIVATION

Take a few moments to connect with your breath and body. If there's any part of your body or being that needs some time, take that time and breathe with it.

Send your breath awareness to your third eye center. Close your eyes and look upward and inward toward the space between your brows.

Assess this energy center. Check in with it. How does the energy feel?

If it feels depleted, drop your forehead into the palms of your hands. See loving energy streaming down from the Source of light into your heart, hands, and then this center. When you feel you've had enough, return your hands to an easy resting position.

Check in with the energy again. What does it need you to know?

If you feel that you've avoided the gifts of this center in the past, take a moment to acknowledge this. Be clear that you're willing to change this now and reclaim your ancient wisdom.

Affirm:

> *I am willing to clear all karmic debts or doubts that have stood between me and my gifts and my experience of ancient wisdom.*

Then invite in the energy of the Golden Ray as follows:

- ✧ Imagine the crown of your head opening up. See golden light energy pouring from the heart of Source, passing through your crown, and washing through your third eye.

✧ See your third eye awakening from slumber. See its energy becoming golden. See it filled with light. See it awakening the light of ancient wisdom within you.

✧ Then make this activating declaration:

> *Thank you, enlightened master Kuthumi, for blessing me with your presence and light.*
>
> *Thank you for upgrading my frequency with the Golden Ray of Wisdom.*
>
> *I welcome in this incredible light, as it activates the gifts and the wisdom I have previously abandoned, rejected, or ignored.*
>
> *I AM filled with the Golden Ray of Source light.*
>
> *I AM activated by the Golden Ray of Source light.*
>
> *I AWAKEN the ancient wisdom of Source light in myself.*
>
> *I AM aligned to the Golden Ray of Source light.*
>
> *Thank you, Kuthumi, for being my spiritual doorkeeper, for protecting me as I awaken the ancient wisdom locked within me.*
>
> *Thank you for guiding me along my path and for helping me reclaim a more visceral and devotional connection with Source, so that I can feel more connected, supported, and aligned with spiritual vision.*
>
> *I AM willing to see the world differently.*
>
> *I AM willing to see the world through the Golden Ray of Source.*
>
> *I AM awakened.*
>
> *I AM activated.*
>
> *I AM aligned.*
>
> *And so it is.*

You are now aligned with the Golden Ray of Source. Do this activation anytime you feel limited in your vision. Kuthumi will be your friend and guide.

MA'AT

Ma'at (pronounced Ma-yet) is an ancient Egyptian goddess associated with truth, harmony, and balance. She first appears during the Old Kingdom and is one of the most ancient forms of the divine goddess of justice. She is depicted as having wings, which are often associated with being in the heavens or being able to watch from above. She is therefore similar to what we now call an angel—a being that is watching over us from above.

The ancient Egyptians had a deep reverence for the gods and knew that a spiritual force of justice was watching over them. Ma'at was that force. She was able to restore balance to the system in a similar way to the workings of karma. It was said that at the time of your death, your soul would be transported to her temple, where she would appear carrying the sacred scales of justice. She would place your life choices on one side of the scales and a divine feather on the other. If the scales were balanced, or tipped to the side of the feather, it would indicate good moral choices and you would continue your journey to the cosmos. If the scales tipped to the side of your life choices, it would indicate poor moral standards and you would be sent to the underworld to seek redemption.

Restorer of Harmony

The energy of Ma'at is powerful and angelic, and when I have connected to her, I have genuinely felt that she is part goddess and part angel. She has a divine golden energy that fills up the space and I see her as an African-style woman with braided hair that is tied up high on her head. She is adorned with golden jewellery and shining jewels. Her eyes are deep brown and gold. She reminds me of a lioness— fierce, graceful, and poised.

Once, when I was in her presence, I heard the words:

I am justice embodied, a restorer of peace.
Call on me and I shall bless your world with harmony once more.

I felt blessed to hear this and I knew that Ma'at's energy was about restoration and peace. She's a divine energetic force that is dedicated to harmony and balance. The story of her scales of justice illustrates that when we make poor moral decisions and lack ethical direction, we can be tormented by the hell of our own conscience.

In the past, Ma'at encouraged her people to live a graceful life and be considerate toward others. Now she encourages us to restore the balance and harmony of our life. She helps us draw down light from Source to completely obliterate pain and to release fear and uncertainty from a situation. For example, if you are having an argument with a loved one or even going through a difficult divorce, this Divine Master of justice will come in, bless everyone involved, and steer the whole situation toward the most harmonious solution possible.

If there's something in your past that you regret, or are haunted by, Ma'at can help you make peace with it and trust that all your experiences have led to the awareness and morality that you hold in your heart today.

Working with Ma'at

Working with Ma'at can help you:

© understand what is the right decision

© restore harmony to a challenging situation

© come through difficult times and legal situations

© trust that your past is the past for a reason

Ma'at's activation is an intentional prayer that activates the energy of harmony. It sends a golden wave of energy to situations both conscious and unconscious, clearing karmic debt and creating space for harmony and healing in your world.

COSMIC HARMONY ACTIVATION

Connect to your breath. Breathe.

If there are any situations, past or present, in your life that you wish to be brought into balance and blessed by harmony, think of them now.

If there are any past decisions that haunt you, experiences that you wish you could have avoided or changed, or parts of your past you are ready to release, review them now. Instead of being pulled into the drama, skim through them quickly, as if you're flicking through old black-and-white photographs.

When you're ready, say:

> Ma'at, cosmic guardian, embodiment of justice,
>
> I call forth your golden presence now.
>
> Thank you for helping me surrender and release all the energies and experiences of my past that could be blocking my experience of harmony and joy today.
>
> Bring unto me your scales of justice and restore peace and harmony to my world.
>
> Thank you for helping me shine the light of forgiveness on myself.
>
> Thank you for helping me change my views of others in situations where I have felt that they have been unjust.
>
> Thank you for helping me find the strength to make the changes I need to make in order to be more aligned with harmony and light.
>
> Thank you for helping me see beyond my ego and the limiting stories it creates within my mind.
>
> Divine Ma'at, break all the chains, cut all the cords, and break down the barriers of fear.
>
> I am ready to experience harmony once more.
>
> I am a bringer of peace.
>
> I love from a space of truth.
>
> I welcome the light of harmony into my world.
>
> And so it is.

When you've finished this activation, light a candle in honor of your past. Let the light represent the wisdom that you have now.

MARY MAGDALENE

According to the Gospels, Mary Magdalene was one of the few women who traveled with Jesus and supported his ministry. Her name means "Mary of Magdala." Magdala was a small fishing town on the western shore of the Sea of Galilee and in those days, a person would often be known by where they were from.

According to the Gospel of Luke, Mary was the woman from whom Jesus drove out seven demons. This story is also told in the Gospel of Mark. In Christian and Gnostic circles, there has been speculation that this meant Mary Magdalene was someone who faced her own "demons," meaning she overcame personal challenges or even mental health issues, which were then considered to be "demonic possession," as there were no psychiatrists or psychologists to support sufferers.

Seer of Angels and Apostle to the Apostles

Whatever the truth of Mary of Magdala's "demons," she was certainly "the Apostle to the Apostles"—the teacher of teachers. The story goes that after the crucifixion, Jesus was laid to rest in a tomb. One morning, Mary went to the tomb and noticed that the rock covering the entrance had been moved to the side. She went inside and could not find Jesus. Instead, there were two angels there, one where Jesus's head had rested and the other where his feet had been. She began to weep.

The angels looked at her with compassion and asked, "Why are you crying?"

Mary responded, "They have taken my teacher. Have you seen my teacher?"

As grief washed over her, she felt a hand on her shoulder and heard someone say her name. She turned around and a man was there, but she did not recognize him.

"Mary," he said.

Then she realized he was Jesus, completely healed and covered in light. She fell to her knees at his feet.

After this, Jesus went on to share a special mission with Mary. He taught her secret knowledge and spiritual information that he asked her to share with the world.

Once she had had her time with the risen Christ, Mary went back to the rest of the disciples to tell them that Jesus had risen and what he had said. At first, many of them were shocked and questioned Mary's authority. Who did she think she was to tell them anything? But Levi said, "The Savior made her worthy, who are we to reject her? If the Savior deemed Mary trustworthy, then she is trustworthy. He loved her more than us." Once they came round, the Apostles went on to spread the Christian gospel under Mary's leadership.

So, Mary Magdalene was proof that women could be spiritual leaders. First of all, she had the capacity to see angels. I believe that when she was in the tomb of Christ, his physical body was there, but his soul had left. The angels activated her divine vision so that she could receive a transmission from the spiritual form of Christ and in turn become the Apostle to the Apostles.

At the time, though, the Holy Land was under Roman rule, and they weren't ready for Jesus's sacred teachings or for women to be spiritual leaders. So, Mary was driven out of the Holy Land. She left on a ship with a girl named Sarah, most likely her daughter, Joseph of Arimathea, who was either Mary's or Jesus's uncle, Mary the mother of Christ, and probably a few others. They landed in the south of France, where Mary set up a hermitage and dedicated herself to spiritual practice for the rest of her days.

Mary Magdalene is a spiritual figure with whom I feel a strong bond. She's a powerful feminist saint, and before I had even learnt her full story, I had a dream in which I was transported to a cave and met by a woman with a red veil, who said, "Welcome to the cave of your heart." Then I woke up.

Mary Magdalene is the teacher of teachers, who lived out her life in a cave so that we don't have to. Just as Christians believe Jesus died to save us, so Mary in some way took a "hit" so that we don't have to. On a spiritual level, her energy is dedicated to helping those of us who are in hiding to emerge from our "cave" and bring our light and our gifts to the world.

Working with Mary Magdalene

Working with Mary Magdalene:

© helps you awaken the teacher within

© encourages you to leave your comfort zone

© gives you the strength and confidence to share your light with the world

© supports the process of forgiveness

If you feel that you have a mission to bring healing and change to the world, Mary Magdalene and her angels will help you. She allows you to dial into the strength that you have gained from all of your previous life experiences in order to continue on and become the teacher that you were born to be.

Mary Magdalene's activation is an intentional prayer to awaken the teacher within. It encourages you to let that teacher emerge and become a light to the world.

TEACHER-AWAKENING ACTIVATION

Connect with your breath.

Take a moment to reflect on the unique gifts and qualities of your soul.

If there's a teacher inside you that you are ready to bring out, focus on it now.

Then call in the Magdalene with the words:

> *Mary Magdalene, seer of angels, Apostle to the Apostles, thank you for enveloping me in your sacred light.*
>
> *Thank you for placing your heart against mine, so that I can connect with the Source of divine love.*
>
> *Today, in your presence, I am willing to remember who I truly am.*
>
> *I choose to reconnect with the divine aspects of my being.*
>
> *I choose to remember and honor my divine vision.*
>
> *I choose to acknowledge and call forth the divine teacher I have within.*

Thank you, Mary of Magdala, for being my guide, and for leading me from the cave of my heart space up and out into the world.

To teach is to learn.

To share is to be sustained.

I awaken the teacher within.

I call forth the divine guide in my heart.

I step onto the path of light.

I awaken the teacher within.

I awaken the teacher within.

Thank you, Mary Magdalene, for leading the way.

I have emerged from the cave.

The teacher within is activated.

And so it is.

Once you emerge from this space, be aware of the messages that will be sent your way. Be open to this guidance.

MOTHER MARY

Mary, the mother of Jesus, or Mary of Nazareth, was a simple woman from the first century who had a divine mission to bring a sacred love to the world. As related earlier, at the time of her death, she didn't just pass away, but was "assumed" into heaven. Her spirit was carried up by angels and she herself became an angelic presence, the queen of the angels.

Although Mary is closely associated with Christianity, particular the Catholic Church, which considers her the most important figure after Jesus, it's important to say that her energy goes beyond the limitations of conventional religion and she will connect with anyone whose heart is open to her sacred love.

Protector of Mothers and Children

As Mary was the mother of Jesus, she's seen as a divine parent who can guard and guide. She has a special bond with mothers and children, but anyone can call on her and, like a motherly figure, she will wrap them in her light. I feel that because so many people venerate her and call upon her in complete faith, her energy is one of the most powerful and protective in all of the heavens.

Mother Mary has a pure heart—her love is divine. It is common for those who connect with her to be overwhelmed and emotional. Every time I connect with her energy or experience her while doing energy work for others, I get highly emotional. It's as if my human self cannot fully comprehend the love that she brings to the Earth. Her love is unconditional—it doesn't matter who you are or what you have done in the past, she will open her heart to you and wrap you in her light.

Sapphire Blue Light

Mary's energy is represented by sapphire blue light and she's one of the keepers of the Sapphire Blue Ray, which is the spiritual energy connected to expressing your will and also experiencing the light and protection of Source. To welcome her into your world, you can imagine yourself enveloped in sapphire light. Don't worry if you haven't connected with her in the past—she won't hold it against you. She is willing to support anyone going forward.

"Do Not Be Afraid" and YES!

One of the most revealing stories about Mary's divine purpose is the Annunciation, when Archangel Gabriel announced the coming of Jesus. Mary was sleeping one night when she was woken by a figure of divine light standing at the bottom of her bed. It was Archangel Gabriel in spiritual form. Gabriel then said, "Do not be afraid, for I am an angel of the Lord." Mary felt the presence of love and listened to what the angel said. Gabriel went on to share Mary's future life, saying she would give birth to a special son and he would be named Jesus and would be known the world over as the king of kings.

When Gabriel had finished showing Mary her life (I believe that this all occurred through an inner vision in which she was taken on a journey into the future), she felt that she did have a say in it all. She could refuse and let it all go, but she didn't. She said, "Let all of what you have just shared be true."

Let's break down this powerful experience. First of all, Mary had a vision of an angel. A divine being showing up unannounced could startle anyone, but when angels arrive, their infinite love washes over us and instantly we feel safe. What Gabriel really meant when telling Mary not to be afraid was: "Do not be afraid of being this powerful."

This is an important lesson. Mary was a woman and she was receiving a personal download from the angelic realm. She would have been taught that angels only appeared to prophets and rabbis, and here she was having this divine encounter. It must have been a surprise. But it was also a lesson for the world: women are worthy of divine encounters; the experiences of women matter.

The next part of the vision is also important because it has influenced spiritual belief the world over. When Gabriel shared the prophecy, Mary instinctively knew that she had a choice. She could refuse. She could ask for an alternative. When it comes to our life path and our life purpose, we always have a choice. If we feel something isn't working for us or isn't in alignment with our greater good, we can ask for an alternative. This is okay. What's more, we can ask for spiritual help if we wish. In fact, unless we ask for it, it cannot intervene.

Working with Mother Mary

Working with Mother Mary can help with:

◎ protection on all levels

◎ improving your connection to angels

◎ finding your spiritual path

◎ embracing your divine right to be powerful

Mother Mary's activation calls down the Sapphire Blue Ray from the heart of Source so you can feel safe and protected as you embrace your divine right to be powerful.

SACRED PROTECTION ACTIVATION

Breathe. Visualize yourself immersed in sapphire blue light.

Welcome in Mother Mary with the words:

> *Divine Mother Mary, mother of God, queen of angels,*
>
> *I welcome your presence into this space.*
>
> *Thank you and your holiest angels for breaking down the barriers, concerns, apprehensions, and other energies that are clouding my energy.*
>
> *Thank you for removing from my energy field any lower vibrations, energies, foreign bodies, or programs that are standing in the way of my greatness.*
>
> *Thank you for embracing me with your love.*

I am filled with divine light and love.

Thank you for drawing around my energy, in every direction, a spiritual force field of light that only welcomes in loving experiences.

I AM protected by the sapphire blue light of Mother Mary.

I AM cherished by the sapphire blue light of Mother Mary.

I AM loved by Mother Mary.

Today I choose not to be afraid.

I awaken my divine power.

I fearlessly step onto the path of light.

I AM the light.

And so it is.

MELCHIZEDEK

Melchizedek (pronounced Mel key zeh dek), whose name means "King of Righteousness," is the first high priest mentioned in the Bible, the one who initiated all the great teachers who followed him. He is mentioned in several Abrahamic texts, including the Dead Sea scrolls, and also the Kabbalistic text the *Zohar*. He is an ancient gatekeeper of the light who is dedicated to helping all those walking the spiritual path to take the initiatory steps to align with the light.

The best way to describe Melchizedek is like a wizard. When you invoke him, it feels as though you are coming into contact with Dumbledore from the Harry Potter books. He is an extremely tall being with long white hair and a long beard, wearing gray, silver, and white robes, and a necklace that has a Merkaba, a three-dimensional six-pointed star, on it. His energy is brilliant and clear—like a breath of fresh air. In his presence, I feel as though I am aligned with miracles and light—he holds the space to make anything possible.

Upon looking into the scriptures and texts that mention Melchizedek, I found that this high priest was well regarded and even considered a previous incarnation of Christ. When I tuned in to his energy to get a deeper understanding, I felt he was in fact a bringer of Christ light to Earth. I genuinely believe that he was preparing the way for the future vehicles of Christ light such as Mary and Jesus. I don't think he was an incarnation of Christ, but he was a great spiritual teacher who, when it came to his physical passing, ascended and, I believe, became a master teacher who helped Jesus take the initiatory steps required to step into his great teaching role. Now he guides all those who want to walk the path less traveled.

The Order of Melchizedek

In the New Testament, Jesus mentions the Order of Melchizedek. This divine order of light beings, angels, and masters is a congregation of energetic forces dedicated to lighting up and outshining all darkness. They are the keepers of the Christ light and Holy Spirit energy. When this is invoked, no darkness can exist and all that is lower in vibration is transformed into light. Archangel Michael is among the angels working within this order of pure light.

The intergalactic and divine members of this order are willing to work with all those who call upon them, to initiate them, and to align them with the highest frequencies. By connecting with this gathering of great beings (*see activation below*), we give permission for our energy to be upgraded by light, so that we can become a greater vessel for light, healing, and purpose in the world.

High Priest of Atlantis and Merlin

Melchizedek has had many initiatory incarnations. He was a high priest in Atlantis and served the Divine Feminine. He also had an incarnation in the British Isles, where he was the master magician Merlin, who held the energies of the Holy Grail and was the spiritual guide to King Arthur and the Knights of the Round Table.

It seems that for many lifetimes Melchizedek has been strongly associated with the energies of light, Christ, and the Divine Feminine. A huge part of his energetic purpose is to bring light to the Earth through those who call on him and to restore a balance between the masculine and feminine energies of the world. Although his presence is very masculine, powerful, and even fierce, he is a devout priest of the feminine energies and is dedicated to helping the world know that we need the feminine principle in order for radical healing to take place across the planet.

Working with Melchizedek

Working with Melchizedek:

© helps with the process of ascension

© guides you to connect with your inner magic

© is incredible for support with any type of ceremonial work or initiation

© helps you remember ancient past lives

LIGHT INITIATION ACTIVATION

This activation will be most powerful if you do it during the brightest part of the day. You are invited to face east and reach out with your palms facing forward (this is the position Melchizedek used when he was initiating priests and priestesses in Atlantis).

Say:

Melchizedek, great father of light, high priest of Atlantis,

*Order of Melchizedek, light-bearers, angelic beings, and
cosmic guides, thank you for enveloping me in your brilliant
crystal-clear light.*

Thank you for imparting your ancient wisdom and knowledge to me.

I welcome your full system upgrades, light codes, and attunements.

*Thank you, spirit of the holiest light, for penetrating my heart and
mind with your presence.*

I am willing to understand the initiations of my past incarnations.

I am willing to invoke and welcome the Christ light into my being.

*I call upon the great light within. I invite this presence to stand at
the forefront of my heart and mind.*

I invoke armor of the holiest light.

I am aligned with the holiest light.

I am protected by the holiest light.

Blessings be upon me, Order of Melchizedek.

I am initiated into this great circle of truth.

Be with me now, O great holy light.

I AM one with the holiest light.

And so it is.

LADY NADA

Lady Nada is a spiritual embodiment of divine love. She is one of the leaders of the Karmic Board and a member of the Council of Light and is dedicated to bringing Christ consciousness to Earth. In the Aura-Soma healing system, Lady Nada's bottle is the divine counterpart to the Christ. Her spiritual mission is to help the human race embody divine love.

Lady Nada is an aspect of Mary Magdalene. Although the energies appear very different, they are one. When I asked my angel guides to explain this connection, they told me that the Magdalene and Nada were two aspects of the same soul who were expressing themselves in different ways because they were multi-dimensional expressions of divine love.

When I tune in to Lady Nada on an energetic level, I see her as a being made of pure golden light with a light pink aura that radiates pure love and acceptance. To me, her appearance is more angelic than that of some of the other masters, who often appear as humans. Having said that, Lady Nada is commonly seen by other practitioners as a light blonde white woman often wrapped in a pink cloak.

Priestess of Atlantis

Lady Nada was a high priestess of Atlantis and those drawn to her are likely to have had incarnations in Atlantis or other ancient civilizations. She gives permission to us all, but particularly to those embracing the feminine in this lifetime, to draw back our power and wholly embrace the sacred aspects of ourselves.

If you feel that you are here to fully unfold the divinely feminine aspects of your soul, Lady Nada will be a light and guide to you. If you feel strongly that you are a priestess or were a priestess in ancient times, working directly with her light can help you retrace the experiences of those incarnations and remember the lessons your soul learnt then. If you are ready to awaken the priestess within, call on Lady Nada now.

Roses and the Blooming Heart

Lady Nada's energy is strongly connected to pink roses. Pink roses have long been associated with love, innocence, femininity, and sweetness. This is the best way to describe the energy that naturally comes into your energy field when Lady Nada is invoked.

To support your connection to Lady Nada, or if you want to strengthen the qualities that she brings to the Earth, you may want to consider the following:

© placing pink roses on your spiritual altar

© putting pink rose petals in the bath

© anointing your chakras with rose oil

© painting a pink rose in bloom

A Leader of the Karmic Board

As one of the leaders of the Karmic Board, which is a congregation of spiritual beings dedicated to implementing the law of cause and effect, Lady Nada has the capacity to help us overcome karmic blockages surrounding the heart. You can call on her for help in healing your heart space and also clearing away patterns that you are carrying in your energy field that are standing in the way of experiencing love.

Karmic blockages are often misunderstood. Many people think that a blockage is punishment from the universe because of bad choices or wrongful behavior, but it's not. The universe is on our side. It wants us to have a positive experience down here on Earth, but it also honors our own choices and experiences.

Karmic blockages can actually be created from innocent choices, for example, continually letting someone's bad behavior or mistreatment of us slide because we really want to see the good in them, or choosing not to let love in because there's a part of us that's scared of the unknown. They are often repeating patterns that are in some way connected to our spiritual blueprint (the journey of our soul so far), usually because an experience in a previous incarnation was so traumatic that the memory (even if we are unaware of it) is stored in our being.

Possible signs of karmic blockages:

- deep-rooted fear of the unknown
- other fears or phobias
- continuous challenges in finding a romantic partner
- feeling misunderstood
- finding it difficult to get close to others

If you want to overcome karmic blockages, the following exercise is great for clearing them.

Call to the Karmic Board to Clear Karmic Blockages

Take some time to center yourself. Breathe deeply.

Tune in to your body. Scan your body.

If there's a part of you that needs extra care or attention, place your hand there now and breathe toward it.

Once your body has become more relaxed, set the intention to bring your spirit to the forefront of your being with a few simple words such as:

I call my spirit to the forefront of my being.

Prepare yourself to release karmic bonds and barriers, and when you're ready, say these words:

I call upon the lords and ladies of karma.

Thank you for bearing witness to this intention and protest.

I declare that I was not born to suffer.

I accept this as my truth now.

I declare that it is my right to experience love in all forms and without conditions.

I accept this as my truth now.

I declare that love is mine to have and to share.

I accept this as my truth now.

Thank you, Karmic Board, for clearing all blockages, debts, unfinished patterns, experiences, psychic pain, or any other barriers that could be standing in the way of my experience of love.

Thank you, Lady Nada, Queen of the Rose, for holding this sacred space.

I welcome your holy golden light. Thank you for honoring me.

I remove all blockages from my being now.

I am unbound, unwound, and free.

It is my divine right to love and be loved.

I am love. I am loving. I am loved.

I accept this as my truth now.

I accept this as my truth now.

I accept this as my truth now.

And so it is.

When you have completed the declaration, spend time in self-care, go into nature, have a bath, or do something else that really nourishes you. Often karmic blockages have been with us for lifetimes and so it takes commitment, focus, and determination to remove them. Once you've put your protest in to the Karmic Board, the energy will begin to disperse, but often self-nourishment is required to really allow all of your being to accept the shift.

To help things along, you may repeat the declaration as often as you wish. If you have experienced hardships in the heart department and really need to "undo" karma, I recommend doing it every day for 40 days and 40 nights.

Working with Lady Nada

Working with Lady Nada:

- ○ helps you connect with your heart space
- ○ supports you in opening up your heart to love
- ○ guides you to recognize the power in vulnerability
- ○ helps you uncover the Divine Feminine aspects within

This activation helps you remove all of the blocks and barriers that stand before your heart. Love is already within you, waiting to be unlocked and shared with the world. This intentional prayer will support you in awakening the higher heart space and embodying the feminine Christ light in the world.

HEART-AWAKENING ACTIVATION

Visualize yourself immersed in golden and light pink light.

Once you are in this divine cloak of light, know that Lady Nada is with you.

Visualize a pink rosebud.

Allow the petals to unfurl before you.

Allow the rose to bloom.

Say:

Lady Nada, Queen of the Rose, high priestess of Atlantis, essence of unconditional love, the divine feminine Christ light,

I welcome your blessings, your love and support.

As I picture the sacred rose blooming in my mind,

I allow my heart space to open.

I claim love as my truth, my being, and my destiny.

Thank you, Nada, for guiding me to see where I have not yet let my love reach.

Wherever I have resisted the presence of love, I welcome it back now.

I allow my heart space to awaken.

I allow my heart space to bloom.

I accept love as my truth.

Thank you for leading the way to my truth.

I welcome your leadership today.

My heart is awakened and activated.

And so it is.

Paul the Venetian

Paul the Venetian, also known simply as "the Venetian," is one of the original masters of the Theosophical Ascended Master teachings. He is a member of the Great White Brotherhood and the guardian of the Rose Pink Ray of the Heart. He is said to be the ascended form of Paolo Veronese, a famous artist of the Italian Renaissance. "The Venetian" refers to the fact that he had links with Venice, Italy, and according to the Ascended Master teachings, on his passing in 1588, Paul, or Paolo, was given the opportunity to share his lifelong wisdom with humanity from a spiritual level.

There are many contrasting ideas about Paul the Venetian in the Ascended Master teachings. C.W. Leadbeater, a prominent member of the Theosophical Society, called him Venetian Chohan, but didn't refer to Paolo Veronese. That information surfaced later from within the Ascended Master movement.

If there is contrasting information out there, whatever the subject, that's okay. What's more important is to trust what you feel and make up your own mind. Personally, for some reason I've always had the clear feeling that there's a Venetian/Venusian link and Paul the Venetian is actually one of the Venusians, a race of beings that are dedicated to bringing light and grace to the world, which is why one of his incarnations was as an Italian artist. (*For the Venusians, see Sanat Kumara and Lady Venus.*)

Paul the Venetian appears as a wise, well-dressed figure. His energy body is filled with light pinks, yellows, and golds. There's a femininity about him and, although he appears human, something very otherworldly. He has grace and poise, and I feel that his gift is in looking after the details and doing things with finesse.

To me, he is a spiritual guide who is dedicated to the divine energy of grace. Grace guides us to do things that will be of service to others. It's the force that helps us tap into our gifts and be sustained by the knowledge that what we do will bring more beauty, connection, and love into the world. If you ever lack inspiration, Paul will open you up to the energy of grace. Here is a message I received from him:

> *I am a devotee of the force of grace.*
> *I am a messenger of divine inspiration.*
> *Open your heart to receive these blessings.*

Working with Paul the Venetian

Working with Paul the Venetian:

- © can help you tap into your creativity
- © will support you in gracefully expressing your gifts
- © opens your heart space to divine inspiration

Paul the Venetian brings waves of good energy, grace, and encouragement. He is a wonderful guide for artists, musicians, designers, and anyone else who needs support channeling their talents. He has a particularly soft spot for anyone who has to use their hands to express their talent. He is therefore a perfect guide for anyone who wants to express their gifts with grace.

If you have a creative idea or you are finding it difficult to share your gifts, either because you feel blocked or are uncertain how to do so, this keeper of the Rose Pink Ray can help you reconnect with your heart space and share who you are without concern.

Paul the Venetian's activation is about allowing grace into your heart space so that you can share the purest, most vulnerable but most powerful aspects of yourself with the world.

EXPERIENCING GRACE ACTIVATION

Close your eyes.

Invoke the Rose Pink Ray with the words:

> *I AM one with the Rose Pink Ray.*
> *I AM aligned with divine love.*
> *I align my being with infinite compassion and self-care.*

Visualize yourself being bathed in rose pink light.

Then say:

> *Paul the Venetian, divine artist, cosmic inspirer, thank you for*
>   *placing your hand upon my heart.*
> *I welcome your gentle and loving presence today.*

Thank you for activating a greater trust of my talents.

Thank you for activating the gifts that I was born to share.

Thank you for activating the light of grace.

I open my being up to the light of grace

I choose to be led by the light of grace

Thank you, Venetian, for opening my heart space, for unlocking the doors and taking down the barriers that I have built within myself. I am ready to live in grace.

I am the light of grace.

I am the light of grace.

I am the light of grace.

And so it is.

LADY PORTIA

L ady Portia is an Ascended Master whose name is Latin for "doorway." She is the twin flame of Saint Germain (*see p.224*) and one of the keepers of the Violet Flame working with lightworkers across the globe to overcome low-vibrational energy and circumstances that could be standing in the way of their great work.

Lady Portia has had many Earthly incarnations in which she has been dedicated to doing what is morally and spiritually right, and while in the spiritual realms, she has appeared to those on Earth to direct the course of karma and justice. Basically, she is the spiritual force behind the energy of justice.

When I connect with Lady Portia, her energy is forthright and powerful. She is an unshakable presence who has both strength and courage. On a psychic level, she has a bright violet and lavender energy field. Originally I saw her as pure cosmic energy, then, when I sent her the message that I was feeling privileged to connect with her, I saw her energy as a human face, with high cheekbones and porcelain skin, and a violet jewel on her forehead. She seemed to be wearing a veil and a flowing robe that were deep violet in color. She felt angelic and loving.

Karma and Justice

Lady Portia is a member of the Karmic Board that regulates the law of cause and effect, and this means she is also strongly connected to the angels of justice (Zadkiel, Holy Amethyst and Raguel). She's a guiding figure, a light being who helps us understand that every action has a reaction, a consequence, some sort of effect on us. It's important to say that most of the time the effect is a positive one. Karma is often misrepresented as a chain of punishment, when in fact it is a spiritual principle that encourages us to make informed choices from the heart, in the knowledge that the positive energy from those choices will bless the path before us.

Lady Portia helps us recognize the impact of our judgments, choices, actions, and non-actions on ourselves and the world. If you've ever felt the need to rethink or retract something because of the negative effects it could have on you, someone you love, or even the world, there's a good chance that the spirit of Lady Portia has come to guide you.

It's important to note, though, that you can't direct karma. Don't wish "bad karma" on people. This has become quite common in today's world, with people often saying things like "Let karma take care of them," but that in itself is an intention that could have karmic repercussions.

Lady Portia and the Karmic Board are dedicated to bringing a sense of awareness and morality to the world. She wants to help those feeling inspired to bring about conscious change, whether it be with social, moral or spiritual issues. One thing she often encourages is seeing things from another person's point of view. She wants everyone to be counted in when changes are made.

Working with Lady Portia

Call on Lady Portia for help with:

© world issues

© human rights

© legal cases or situations, or anything regarding contracts

© guiding political leaders to do the right thing

© transforming social constructs that limit or hurt others

Divine Order

Lady Portia is the guiding force of divine order. Whenever a situation gets out of hand or is beyond our control, we can ask her to bring in healing light and divine order.

Divine order is the force that corrects unjust situations and energies that are working against the greater good of all beings. It can correct a system that is oppressing or harming an individual or group. The key to working with the energy of divine order is asking to be guided to take the action that can lead to change. It's not just about praying and hoping something will shift, it's about being open to listening to the oppressed and taking steps that lead to healing. Of course we can continue seeking justice in the way we feel is best, but it's important to be led by those who have been affected the most and to trust that the universe is supporting the healing and correction.

When you call in divine order with this activation, Lady Portia and her spirit of justice will help you see things from a higher perspective and take the right steps to restore order.

DIVINE ORDER ACTIVATION

Settle down and breathe deeply.

Ask yourself these questions:

✧ Where in my life do I feel something is or was unjust?

✧ Where have I tried to direct the spiritual law of karma because I felt attacked?

Take a moment to reflect. Allow whatever comes up to come up. Whatever rises to the surface is what is ready to be changed.

Visualize yourself immersed in lavender and violet light, the energy of transformation.

Say:

> Lady Portia, goddess of justice, thank you for helping me welcome the power and presence of divine order into my life.
>
> In this moment I surrender to you any negative thoughts, bonds, connections, or ideas that could be standing in the way of my growth.
>
> I am ready to be led by the light.
>
> I step into the Violet Flame of Justice,
>
> I release karmic bonds that hold me as a victim.
>
> I call back my power.
>
> I claim my light and truth.

Thank you, Lady Portia, for helping me upgrade my thoughts so that I can operate from the heart and see the other person's point of view.

Thank you, for helping me make informed decisions from a space of truth and goodness.

I am guided by the Violet Flame.

I am protected by the Violet Flame.

I am honored by the Violet Flame.

And so it is.

QUAN YIN

Quan Yin (sometimes Kuan Yin) is a bodhisattva, a being of pure compassion, and the goddess of mercy, compassion, and love. She is loved the world over, especially in the East, in China, Korea, Japan, and Malaysia.

Quan Yin was one of the first Ascended Masters I learnt about on my spiritual journey. As I mentioned earlier, I was introduced to her through my Reiki training. For this reason I have always strongly associated her with energy healing. It seems to me that she is ready and willing to work with anyone on a healing journey, either as a practitioner or as a person seeking physical and emotional wellbeing.

There is something very gentle and sacred and approachable about Quan Yin. Connecting with her energy feels effortless. She reminds me somewhat of Mother Mary, but her energy is much softer and gentler. It feels as though every step she takes and every move she makes has poise and grace. When I connect with her, she reminds me of the gracefulness of Asian culture—of the politeness and poise you find there. When you see images and statues of Quan Yin, you often see her holding pearls, which represent purity, wisdom, and illumination. You may also see her holding a bowl of rice or a sacred vase, showing her desire to give and to feed others with her light and love.

Bodhisattva

Quan Yin, like Green Tara (*see p.140*), is a bodhisattva, an enlightened and compassionate being. Bodhisattvas are part of the Buddhist tradition, but they remind me of the Western concept of angels. I see angels as divine beings who are one with Source, but express themselves in an individual way so that they can help those who are ready to connect with them. Just like angels, bodhisattvas can be role models as well as divine guardians, inspiring us to live from a heart-centered space. In many lineages of Buddhism, practitioners focus on acting like bodhisattvas and, as mentioned earlier, it is believed that a great practitioner can become a bodhisattva at the time of their mortal death, just as in other traditions it is believed an evolved soul can become an Ascended Master.

Compassion Goddess

Not only is Quan Yin a female buddha and an enlightened being, she's a goddess figure, a representation of the power of creation in female form. She is all about encouraging us to offer care, forgiveness, and compassion, first to ourselves and then to others. She helps us remember that we are all love.

If you're finding it difficult with someone at the moment, the best way you can move forward is to go beyond wanting to understand why they are the way they are. Move beyond their behavior and mistakes and the challenges of the relationship. If you're finding it challenging with someone you love, call on Quan Yin and ask her to bless the other person with her love and to help you to be compassionate toward yourself.

Working with Quan Yin

Working with Quan Yin can help with:

© developing grace and poise

© feeling compassionate toward yourself and others

© stepping back from a situation that's causing you distress

© improving your own self-care

Quan Yin's activation is about drawing the light of the bodhisattvas to you. These bright lights of Buddhism represent ultimate compassion and grace. Though experiencing them more deeply, you are encouraging yourself to become more like them.

BODHISATTVA ACTIVATION

Breathe deeply.

If there's a challenging situation between you and another person, think of it now.

Imagine pure pearly white energy washing over you and the situation gently like summer rain.

Say:

> Quan Yin, divine mother of compassion,
> I welcome your light. I welcome your grace.
> Thank you for wrapping me in your energy with care.

In your presence, I surrender all the situations in my life that are causing me concern and stress.

Thank you for gently guiding the situations in my life toward compassion and understanding. I am ready to welcome change now.

Thank you for awakening the aspects of my being that can be more compassionate.

Thank you for awakening the aspects of my being that can have more grace and understanding.

I welcome your guidance on where I can have more poise.

I welcome your guidance on where I can be more careful.

I welcome your guidance on where I can allow my heart to open.

Thank you for surrounding me in the light of the brightest bodhisattvas.

I set the intention to become a more graceful being.

I AM the light of grace.

I set the intention to become more forgiving with my heart.

I AM the light of forgiveness.

I set the intention to become a brighter light.

I awaken the bright one within.

What I see in you, I choose to see in myself.

And so it is.

Bring your hands to your heart and hold them together in prayer for a moment.

When you feel you have received what you need, bow in respect to Quan Yin and know she is bowing in respect to you.

SAINT GERMAIN

S aint Germain is short for the Comte de Saint Germain (the Count of Saint Germain), who was an 18th-century European adventurer and alchemist. This spiritual luminary is connected with the original Ascended Master teachings and is a master to whom many feel connected the world over.

Although evidence shows that Saint Germain actually existed, in fact rubbed shoulders with some of the most elite members of European society, his real name and background are shrouded in mystery. It is said that he claimed to be the son of the Hungarian nobleman Francis II Rákóczi. Although no proof exists, it could be possible. Putting what I have read together with what I can sense about Saint Germain's human experience, it seems likely that he was the product of an illicit affair between two high-profile individuals, most likely royals. So, he was given the title of count, a good education, and all the financial wealth he needed to have a "good life," but he was denied any formal connection to his real parents and may not even have known who they were.

Man of Miracles

Saint Germain was acknowledged as a man of miracles because he was a noted alchemist and magician and apparently never aged. At one point he claimed to be over 500 years old, though this was most likely a joke.

He was probably a member of the Rosicrucian Order and a Freemason, which would tie in nicely to his capacity to keep secrets, and was definitely, according to the evidence, an amazing entertainer who wowed his audiences with stories, demonstrations of magic, and even telepathy. His natural charm helped him find his place in the world, and I get the impression that the lack of a strong family connection was what sent him around Europe searching for answers and rubbing shoulders with royalty in England, France, and the Netherlands.

Founding Figures

As an Ascended Master, Saint Germain is one of the founding figures of the Ascended Master teachings and is connected to many schools of thought in Theosophy. In fact many teachers in this movement have claimed to have met with him. Helena Blavatsky and Annie Besant both made this claim, and Guy Ballard, the founder of the "I AM" Activity (*see p.18*), shares in the opening of his book *Unveiled Mysteries* that he met Saint Germain at the foot of Mount Shasta in the 1930s and was initiated into the mysteries by him. I personally feel that even though these teachers have "met" with Saint Germain, these encounters are likely to have been on a spiritual/mental/telepathic level, and therefore something that we're all able to experience through meditation.

Saint Germain is in fact a spiritual guide to anyone who is ready to experience transformation in their life. When I see him on a clairvoyant level, he is a well-dressed man with olive skin, a goatee beard, and a mustache. He will often be wearing a uniform that looks regal and may even appear wrapped in a violet and gold cloak. He is strongly associated with the color violet, amethyst crystals, and spiritual alchemy. As he was well educated and rubbed shoulders with highly influential people, he's an amazing master to call on if you're going to be attending an important meeting or connecting with people from different backgrounds or going somewhere out of your comfort zone. He will support you and help you feel comfortable, be graceful, and have poise.

Saint Germain's twin flame has been acknowledged as Lady Portia, the goddess of justice (*see p.215*), and he has been strongly associated with Archangel Zadkiel and his twin flame, Holy Amethyst, the angelic presences who guard the Violet Flame.

The Violet Flame

In recent times, Saint Germain has been widely associated with The Violet Flame, a spiritual energy of transmutation and transformation, most likely because he has been acknowledged as the Chohan, or guardian, of the Violet Ray. In the original Ascended Master teachings and the "I AM" Activity, the Violet Flame is considered a spark of greatness and extension of God's heart energy. It helps those in the Earthly realm transform negative energy and overcome anything that's creating discord. The idea is that when we visualize a situation, or even ourselves, being surrounded by the Violet Flame, we are burning away old karmic bonds and creating space for new energies.

From my perspective, the Violet Flame is an energetic retreat space that we can visit in meditation, dreams, and prayer. On my own personal journey, I've often been transported to a place I call the Halls of Learning, which is a school or college on the spiritual planes where initiations take place and we can develop our spiritual skills. I have been taken to a room that is violet in color and has a gigantic fire pit in the center with a roaring violet-colored fire. During my time there, I've met masters and angels, including Saint Germain, and I've been invited to place situations that have been causing me concern onto the flame.

It's important to say that the Violet Flame is an energy of transmutation, which means it doesn't burn away a situation, it transforms it. It is ultimately a flame of alchemy, taking what is heavy, leaden, and burdening and transforming it into something lighter, golden, and liberating.

I love the idea of the Violet Flame because it really gives us an opportunity to take a situation that is worrying us and to make space within our heart and mind for a miracle. In my work I have led audiences through Violet Flame meditations in which I have called in Saint Germain. You, too, can be taken to the Violet Flame in meditation or, if you find that difficult, you can visualize yourself being surrounded by violet fire and welcome in the benefits of transmutation and transformation. Or you can try the activation below!

Working with Saint Germain

Call on Saint Germain to help you:

©   transform the energy of a situation

©   overcome family dramas or karma

©   move beyond limiting beliefs or stories

©   become the leader you have within

VIOLET ALCHEMY ACTIVATION

This activation supports you in drawing down the energy of the Violet Flame to burn away any karmic blocks or concerns that may be standing between you and greatness. Through this work you can transmute and transform all stuck energy into energy that will support your spiritual transcendence.

Connect with your breath.

If there is an aspect of your life that you are ready to transform, think of it now.

If you don't know what you need to transmute in order to grow, be open to direction.

Set the intention that you are ready to transmute and transform any old patterns, ideas, stories, or limiting beliefs that could be holding you back. Know that you have the capacity to heal and change.

Visualize yourself putting on a violet cloak. See your whole auric field becoming violet.

As the violet energy fills your field, see it beginning to take any energy that looks heavy, stuck, or leaden and transform it into light, flowing, golden energy.

See your field becoming violet with glints of gold all around.

Say:

> *Thank you, keepers of the Violet Flame, for wrapping me in a violet cloak of transformation. I welcome your guidance, support, and divine alchemy at this time.*

Wait until you feel the energy shift, then say:

> *Thank you, Saint Germain, Master of the Violet Flame, for coming into my energy field at this time.*
>
> *Thank you for using your sacred spiritual alchemy to transmute and transform all the energy in my energy field that is old, heavy,*

stuck, leaden, and restrictive into energy that is fresh, light, flowing, and golden.

I am ready to make energetic shifts in my being, to move beyond the limiting stories and write new ones.

I am ready to embody the power and presence of love in all aspects of my being.

Thank you for clearing the karmic bonds that hold me in fragility.

Thank you for showing me the parts of myself I am ready to leave behind so that I can become who I truly am.

Thank you for clearing the path to my greatest good.

I am ready to experience my greatest good.

I am committed to my greatest good.

I invoke the Violet Flame.

I am one with the Violet Flame.

I AM the Violet Flame.

I welcome all energetic upgrades. Thank you, Saint Germain, for conducting them now.

I am grateful for your support.

I am transformed.

And so it is.

SANAT KUMARA

Sanat Kumara, whose name is Sanskrit for "Eternal Youth," is an advanced cosmic light being who is dedicated to helping the Earth rise up toward the light. As far as I'm concerned, he's one of the leaders of the Ascended Masters. I'm not certain this congregation of souls has an actual hierarchy, but I definitely feel a commanding presence when this master's energy comes into my space.

Legend has it that Sanat Kumara came from Venus 6.5 million years ago and is eternally 16 years old, due to the atmospheric differences between the two planets. In Theosophical teachings, "Lord" Sanat Kumara is the "regent" of Earth and of humanity, the head of the spiritual hierarchy that governs, guides, and supports the Earth. Much of the information about him states that he resides upon the etheric planes in Shambhala, the incredible city floating in a space between this dimension and the next.

Sage of the East

Just like angels, Divine Masters have appeared in different forms across the world, and Sanat Kumara is no exception. He features in both Buddhism and Hinduism. There is a Buddhist temple in the far north of Kyoto, Japan, called Kurama-dera that was built around AD772 as a shrine to Sanat

Kumara "the Defender Lord." I have made it a goal to visit this temple in the not too distant future.

One time I was speaking to the Japanese translator of one of my oracle decks and she spoke about Sanat Kumara and mentioned that he had "landed" in Kyoto. I really loved that idea. I imagined him just stepping off a starship from a faraway star system. Maybe he did.

In Hinduism there are several mentions of a being called Sanatkumara (all one word). In this tradition he is one of the four mystic sages who were born from the mind of the creator god, Brahma. Legend has it that these sages roamed the land with one intention: to teach. Other texts, such as the *Bhagavata Purana*, suggest that the Kumaras are *bhatkas*, beings of great devotion who have been liberated from birth and who dedicate themselves to serving humanity.

Light-bringer

Some of these ancient texts have clearly influenced our modern understanding of Sanat Kumara. The common theme is that he was born or created directly from the mind of God, or, in my own language, is an extension of the divine mind. If you were to imagine the universe creating light in the form of beings, Sanat Kumara certainly would be one of them. He has been called a bodhisattva, *bhatka*, and a spiritual guide, and in my honest opinion they are all the same thing expressed in different ways. What I've come to feel from all that I've learnt about him is that he is an ancient being who has had several lifetimes in different places on Earth, all ultimately to bring light.

Connecting with Sanat Kumara in meditation has inspired me greatly. I remember meditating one night and connecting with my higher chakras.

I have this process where with each and every breath I draw the power of the stars and the cosmos down through my Stellar Gateway chakra. That night I was seeing myself suspended in the center of the universe, surrounded by the light of the stars. Before me was an incredible being. He was tall and slender, his skin was made of blinding yellow-gold light, his eyes were filled with the same light, and even though there was an androgynous look about him, he was radiating masculine energy. His aura was filled with light pink and yellow energy and he, too, was suspended in the stars. From him, I received some sort of light transfusion. It was intense, but I felt safe. Before our meeting ended, I heard, "I am the keeper of the light." This inspired me to create my bestselling oracle deck *Keepers of the Light*.

The Venusians

It has become widely accepted in spiritual circles that Sanat Kumara is a master from Venus. I agree with this, as when I connect with him, I feel that he is a leading light, along with his twin flame, Lady Venus, of a cosmic race of beings known as the Venusians.

Venus is the second planet from the sun. Named after the Roman goddess of love and beauty, in astrology it represents love, romance, and relationship, but on a spiritual, vibrational level, it represents a higher, unconditional love. Like Sanat Kumara himself, ultimately it's a bringer of light.

The Venusians are a group of beings whose energy feels angelic. Their auras are light pink and gold and they look similar to the beings in the movie *Cocoon*. They have a deep love for the Earth and all its inhabitants. Their divine mission is to inspire the restoration of community, connection, communication, and respect on the planet.

Working with Sanat Kumara

Working with Sanat Kumara:

◎ helps us align with our divine mission

◎ supports us in connecting with higher energy

◎ guides us to connect with our own light

◎ can help us work with other dimensions

Sanat Kumara's activation is a reclamation of the light you were born to be. Before you were here, in this body, you were a star shining high in the heavens. When you call on Sanat Kumara and his angelic Venusian Command, you are held in an energetic cocoon and embraced by light once more.

LIGHT ACTIVATION

Close your eyes. Send deep breaths down to the soles of your feet.

Imagine roots of light coming from the soles of your feet and going down into the heart of the Earth.

Anchor your roots to a copper star at the center of the Earth.

Breathe deeply toward your Earth Star chakra. Feel held. Stabilized. Strong.

Now let your breath reach up and out.

See your crown chakra opening and light streaming from it, shining high into the midnight sky.

Above your crown, see your Soul Star chakra as a multi-dimensional Merkaba star swirling in magenta light.

Imagine the light of your crown sending light wires of connection toward the Merkaba star.

Plug your connection into your Soul Star chakra.

A portal of light opens above your Soul Star and a Milky Way of starlight surrounds your aura.

You have connected directly to your Stellar Gateway.

Through that gateway, you can welcome Sanat Kumara by chanting (either internally or out loud):

SAAAAAH NAAAAAT KUUUUU MAAAA RAAAAA

Thank you, Sanat Kumara, for drawing close to me at this time.

I welcome your leadership and support.

I am ready to remember my truth.

I am willing to be activated by light at a deep cellular level.

It feels so good to know that you are here, leading the way with your eternal acceptance and love.

Thank you, Sanat Kumara, for holding the space for me to access the ancient wisdom I hold within.

I am willing to remember.

I recognize the power of my intention.

I unlock my truth. May it be revealed in the perfect time–space sequence.

I breathe in the light of Source.

I light up on a cellular level.

I welcome the light of Source.

Every choice I make is aligned with the highest good.

I am embraced by the light of Source.

I AM the light.

And so it is.

SERAPIS BEY

Serapis Bey is one of the original masters of the Ascended Master teachings and a member of the Great White Brotherhood. He is seen as the Divine Master who is responsible for ascension.

He is associated with Serapis, a divine being who is said to have unified the Greeks and the Egyptians in harmony and peace. He was traditionally depicted as Greek in appearance, but with an Egyptian headdress and breastplate as a symbol that he was to bring these two nations together. A temple of Serapis is mentioned in historical texts dating back to 323BCE. So, was Serapis an Egyptian god who was adopted by the Greeks? Or a Greek god who was adopted by the Egyptians? We aren't sure. What is evident is that he was able to bring "two worlds together," and that is one of many reasons why Serapis Bey is seen as the Divine Master who is able to support the ascension process.

According to the Ascended Master teachings, Serapis Bey was a priest or spiritual practitioner during the time of Atlantis, and like many spiritually aware beings who were consciously living connected to Source, he fled the land before it was hit by a cataclysm. Like many of the Atlanteans, he went to Egypt, where it is said he chose to incarnate several times as a priest. It is even rumored he became Pharaoh Amenhotep III, the pharaoh who has the most statues and busts surviving to this day.

As someone who's deeply interested in ancient mysteries, I often wonder whether, like the ancient yogis of India, Serapis Bey didn't actually reincarnate but, because he had ascended, lived for many, many lifetimes dedicated to sharing the great work and teachings of the Atlanteans, similarly to Thoth (*see p.248*).

Ascension Chamber

Serapis Bey appears to me not as a normal human, but as a being of light. He dresses as an Egyptian or Atlantean priest would, but radiates a brilliant clear and rainbow light. When I connect with him, I am transported to a temple, which feels as though it is within a pyramid of power. I get the impression that this sacred ethereal retreat is an ascension chamber and that many spiritual practitioners have visited throughout the ages to receive transmissions and codes to facilitate their own ascension process. When I am in this chamber, all the lights go out and I am suspended in complete darkness. I hear the simple message, "You cannot shine without darkness", and then the light is restored. I feel that Serapis Bey is the spiritual being who helps spiritual practitioners trust in their own light.

The ascension process isn't about leaving the body, but arriving fully in the body, as mentioned earlier. Until the end of our mortal life, we are encouraged to shine light on darkness, but the darkness isn't bad, it is simply the parts of ourselves we haven't yet understood or taken the time to get to know. Serapis Bey knows from his time in Atlantis what it's like when people abuse their power or avoid aspects of their spiritual selves, and now he dedicates himself to supporting the evolution of human consciousness from the higher realms.

He is the guardian of the Crystalline Ray. This energy isn't crystal clear, but rainbow. It holds the healing properties of all the colors of the rainbow. By connecting with Serapis Bey, we can invoke this energy. It is like an energetic car wash that washes away all the energies that could be holding us back from being the light we were born to be.

Working with Serapis Bey

Working with Serapis Bey can help with:

- ◎ trusting in your own light and path

- ◎ getting through a challenging time

- ◎ walking the path of ascension

- ◎ embodying and shining your light

Serapis Bey's activation takes you energetically to his ascension chamber so that you can receive a transmission of light to support you in embodying your light and living in an ascended way.

ASCENDED AWARENESS ACTIVATION

First of all, invoke the Crystalline Ray as follows.

Breathe. Visualize yourself immersed in crystal-clear and rainbow light.

Affirm:

> *I AM one with the Crystalline Ray.*
>
> *I AM one with the miraculous.*
>
> *I align with divine clarity and the ascended self.*

When you feel the shift in frequency, say this intentional prayer:

> *Serapis Bey, Atlantean priest, ascended light, thank you for transporting me energetically to your ascension chamber.*
>
> *I welcome your transmission of light into my being.*
>
> *Thank you for unlocking, decoding, and revealing the light I hold within.*
>
> *I step into ascended awareness.*
>
> *I step onto the path of ascended being.*
>
> *I choose to live from a state of heightened awareness.*
>
> *I welcome a transference of ancient and sacred knowledge, information, and insights that can help me have an upgraded experience of life.*
>
> *I choose to unlock all the past-life awareness and ancient wisdom encoded in my soul.*
>
> *I am willing to see my light.*
>
> *I am willing to be embraced by my light.*
>
> *I am consumed by light itself.*
>
> *Thank you, Serapis Bey, for leading the way in light.*
>
> *And so it is.*

LORD SHIVA

L ord Shiva is one of the key deities in Hinduism. His name means "auspicious one." He is sometimes is called *Mahadeva*, "Great God," and is part of the Hindu trinity, along with Brahma, the creator, and Vishnu, the preserver. Shiva is known as the destroyer, for he is seen as the powerful protective force of the universe. In recent times, he has been known as the transformer, because he can be called on to transform a negative situation.

Shiva has many forms, each with its own personality. One of my favorites is Nataraja, "Cosmic Dancer," an agile man with four arms, dancing with one leg up, chest proud, in a wheel of fire. The purpose of this form, and Shiva's main purpose, is to destroy a weary universe and prepare the way for Brahma to begin the process of creation. In a spiritual context, he is the force we can call on for help in busting through the blockages and challenges of our journey and clearing the way for future growth. Shiva can help us move into a new beginning.

He is the divine consort of Kali-Ma (*see p.176*) and, like her, is seen as a wrathful deity because of his fiery, destructive nature, but the truth is that he is a being of unconditional love, and when we invoke his presence or get to know his energy, he will hold us in his arms like a protective father.

Shiva's Symbols

If you've ever seen images of Shiva, you might want to know what all of the symbols or items he is connected to mean. They're actually very lovely and enhance his image.

- At the crown of his head, he often has a crescent moon, a symbol of peace and calm, and of the feminine.

- The trident he carries is a symbol of protection, the three spokes representing the Hindu trinity and three powers: knowledge, desire, and implementation.

- Around his neck, he often has a snake. This represents his ego. He wears it like a jewel, showing he is not governed by fear.

- In one hand he holds a drum, in honor of music, and in the other hand a sun disc, representing light and life.

- Sometimes he'll have prayer beads in a hand or round his neck. These represent purity.

- Finally, Shiva often sits upon a tiger rug, representing the fact that he is aware of the wild but not controlled by it, as he is sitting there strong and composed.

I feel these symbols really help us tap into the energy of Shiva. He's an incredible Divine Master who can help us move beyond the limitations of fear and be composed, strong, and powerful.

In India, I had the honor of staying for a month in a town called Tiruvannamalai, which is host to a holy site dedicated to Shiva. There is a temple called Annamalaiyar, which is at the foot of a holy hill called Arunachala, where Shiva is said to manifest in spiritual form. I walked up the hill with a group of other pilgrims. We started first thing in the morning, and almost two hours later, there we were on the top. When you're almost at the top, you are encouraged to take your shoes off, and you'll meet a group of devotees who walk the hill daily, barefoot, to honor Shiva. Supposedly, when you walk barefoot, you connect with the footsteps of Lord Shiva himself. There's a pair of feet marked out on the top of the hill, so you can honor the feet of Shiva.

Working with Shiva

Working with Shiva can help you:

◎   clear the path ahead

◎   overcome the fears and wickedness of your ego

◎   stay composed in times of anger and challenge

◎   dance with the universe in trust

Shiva's activation incorporates an Indian chant to draw his energy to you. It clears the way so that you can follow your path to the light.

COSMIC CLEARING ACTIVATION

Start by connecting to your breath. Then chant:

Shiva, Shiva, Shiva, Shambo, Mahadeva *Shambo,*

Shiva, Shiva, Shiva, Shambo, Mahadeva *Shambo,*

Shiva, Shiva, Shiva, Shambo, Mahadeva *Shambo.*

Bring your hands to your heart space. Visualize golden light surrounding you. Draw down the divine presence of Lord Shiva with the words:

> *Lord Shiva, cosmic dancer, divine transformer, thank you for blessing me with your divine presence.*
>
> *It is an honor to connect with you in your most infinite and enigmatic form.*
>
> OM nama Shivaya *[OM: oneness, the connecting vibration of the universe; Nama: to honor, to respect, and unite with; Shivaya: Shiva, the great cosmic guide], thank you for clearing my path.*
>
> *I welcome your wisdom into my heart and mind.*
>
> *Thank you for bringing my awareness to the thoughts, feelings, ideas, and beliefs that are holding me back from stepping onto the path of truth.*
>
> *Thank you for guiding me to rise beyond the wickedness of my ego and for helping me know the difference between fear and guidance.*
>
> *I welcome your guiding presence.*
>
> *Bless my energy, Lord Shiva.*
>
> *I welcome your protection, your light, and your guidance.*
>
> *The path ahead is clear.*
>
> *I move forward, guided by light.*
>
> *I dance with the Oneness of the universe.*
>
> *Thank you, Guru Devo, thank you.*
>
> *And so it is.*

Visualize a bright light clearing your path. The *Mahadeva* is leading the way.

Sopdet, Queen of Sirius

Sopdet is the ancient Egyptian name for the star Sirius, one of their most important stars. The goddess Sopdet is its feminine personification. Her name in hieroglyphics can be translated as "triangle" or "sharp one." In Greek she's called Sothis, which again is the name for Sirius. She has been depicted in many forms, most often as a woman wearing a white crown topped by a star, although sometimes she has an elongated head or headpiece. She often appears with Isis, another queen of heaven (*see p.164*).

Sirius

Sirius is the brightest star in the sky and was of utmost importance to the ancient Egyptians. In fact our current New Year was celebrated as "the coming of Sopdet," as during the last week of December, Sirius can be found high in the sky between midnight and dawn.

This bright star is a mysterious one. There is a famous book called *The Sirius Mystery* by Robert Temple that presents the idea that the Dogon people of Mali in West Africa were once in contact with beings from the Sirius star system. What's interesting is that the Dogon people have a tribal diagram with the path of Sirius A, the brightest star in the sky, and its white dwarf companion, Sirius B, which is not visible to the naked eye and wasn't discovered until 1862. Do they know about it because beings visited them from that star system? And is it possible that the ancient Egyptians too, were in touch with the beings from Sirius and that Sopdet wasn't "just" a deity but a personal contact they had in the stars?

Starpeople

I genuinely believe that the Sirius star system is the home of a race of humanoid beings who are most likely living in a dimension higher than our own. I believe that, just like angels, these beings can be contacted through meditation and spiritual practice. Tuning in to them, I have received many impressions and downloads and have come to understand that their light is a bright electric blue and Sopdet is their queen and high priestess. In a similar way to Hathor and the Hathors (*see p.145*) and Lady Venus and the Venusians (*p.255*), she governs the Sirians and guides them on their cosmic mission.

As these beings are from the brightest star in the sky, their mission is to bring great light to the Earth. I was given the impression that in fact many of them are now incarnating upon the Earth as lightworkers. These people will feel called and connected to the stars. Just hearing the name "Sirius" will make them feel connected and they may have the sense that they are remembering home. Often starpeople, of all kinds, are born feeling somehow out of place and that they don't belong. They find themselves "spacing out," dreaming about lands far away from here. With that being said, they came here for a purpose, and through remembering their starry origins, many of them will be able to reconnect with the mission that they are here to fulfill.

When I tried to connect to Sopdet's energy and asked her to come through, I wasn't able to make a direct connection with her and I felt the reason for this was that I was not from her star system. It wasn't that she was judging or abandoning me, more that she was dedicated to her people and their mission. Her vibration felt very high and I could tell her alignment was with peace. I then asked my guides to explain that I was a messenger who was dedicated to bringing awareness to others, and that many of those who connect with my work might be her people. She made way and I was shown an image of a tall woman, made of infinite light, sitting on a throne made of stars and wearing a crown of incredible light. She was a true queen of heaven and felt all-powerful.

Working with Sopdet

Working with Sopdet helps you:

- find light in darkness
- develop a connection with your star power
- remember your cosmic origin
- connect with starpeople guides

If you feel strongly called to connect to Sirius and its star beings, you will feel called to find this star in the midnight sky and experience the feeling of being home once again.

Wherever you are from, Sopdet's activation will beam up your energy and allow you to be surrounded by infinite light.

STARLIGHT ACTIVATION

This activation is best done at night and outside. If you can locate Sirius in the sky, down by Orion's right foot, the dog star following the hunter, gaze at it and set the intention of connecting with the starpeople of Sirius. Then call them in with the words:

> *Sopdet, Queen of Sirius, star beings of Sirius, thank you for sending your wave of electric blue light my way.*
>
> *Thank you for activating the Sirian starlight frequency within my being.*
>
> *I am ready to be aligned with the brightest star in the sky.*
>
> *I remember my purpose and the mission of my soul.*
>
> *Thank you for helping me track down and remember information about my soul's journey on Earth and the origins of my soul.*
>
> *I call down the light of the stars.*
>
> *I bathe in the light of the stars.*
>
> *I am one with the light of the stars.*
>
> *O bright one, Sopdet, queen of heavenly light, thank you for placing your blessing on my being and for guiding me on my way.*
>
> *I choose to remember the truth of my soul.*
>
> *I claim my cosmic identity.*
>
> *And so it is.*

Take some time to receive the light of the stars, and over the next few days and weeks continue to go outside and receive downloads directly from the cosmos.

THOTH

Thoth (pronounced with a silent "h," Toth), also known as Tehuti, is the ancient Egyptian ibis-headed god of writing, divine magic, and the moon. Acknowledged as the sacred scribe who created writing, he is considered to be the great mind behind hieroglyphics and the maintainer of the Egyptian universe.

In the Western magical community, Thoth is seen as an all-powerful spiritual guide who can help us understand the energy of magic and the power of our will. He is the mastermind behind the Hermetic texts (*see below*). The ancient Greeks knew him as Hermes Trismegistus, which means "Hermes Thrice Great," and the Romans as Mercury.

Overall, this divine being has had many incarnations and assumed many forms on Earth. He is all about communication, on all levels, but in particular between our world and the Divine. Divine magic is about creating a connection between heaven and Earth. It's about harnessing the energies of above and below, helping us recognize that we have an infinite inner connection with all, and ultimately Source.

Tuning in to Thoth is a wonderful experience. The best way to describe the energy that comes forth is that of a grandfather. He brings in the energy of safety and feels like a magical guide with lots of stories to tell. At first when I started to connect with him, he arrived in a similar way to an angel: I could see golden and emerald light, but although I could feel a presence, I couldn't see a physical being. Instead, there was an energetic connection and an internal voice that said softly, "I am one with infinite intelligence, beyond all physical states of being, one with the Source of creation." Then I saw a dark-skinned Egyptian man with a long skull, shaved at the front but with what could only be dreadlocks coming from the back. He had golden paint on his forehead and was clad in ceremonial robes, but had his chest bare. He seemed to be involved in some sort of ceremony, but the scene changed as we moved from temple to temple, sacred site to sacred site, Egypt to Atlantis. I realized Thoth was showing me his many incarnations on Earth.

To me, it feels as though Thoth, the man with many names and many incarnations, has become somewhat angelic. He's a light being, a multi-dimensional spiritual guide willing to work with all who are ready to move to the next level of their spiritual development. Working with Thoth isn't for the faint-hearted, for he will reveal all the aspects of our life and world that could be preventing us from progressing. But he's a powerful spiritual ally who helps us attune to the frequencies of divine magic so that we can harness the support of the cosmos.

As he's a divine guide of heaven and Earth, the best way to describe Thoth is as a cosmic light being who can take many forms but prefers to work through telepathic inspiration and visions.

Atlantis

It is said that Thoth was a priest-king of Atlantis. So not only was he a spiritual advisor to the people of Atlantis, he was also their leader. What

I have come to understand from connecting to his energy is that he tried to lead in a loving way. He was firm but very fair. Many of the Atlanteans, however, didn't obey the spiritual laws that Thoth shared with them. He tried to guide them, but he knew that he could never force them to find the balance between Earthly pleasures and devotion to the light, because they had free will.

According to legend, Thoth knew that Atlantis would face repercussions for the abuse of spiritual and psychic powers, and he prepared to evacuate, saving only the most essential spiritual teachings, including the *Emerald Tablet* (*see below*). He fled to Africa and eventually found himself in Egypt, where he buried his knowledge in the land, the temples, and the many students he initiated.

The Soul Lessons of the Atlanteans

The Atlanteans who followed Thoth's primary teachings of spiritual integrity and light are now a congregation of evolved souls who, like angels, work with Thoth to guide those who are open to connecting with them. They specialize in helping those who are finding it difficult to rise beyond aspects of their life that are holding back their spiritual progress. They can help us enjoy Earthly pleasures in a way that is respectful and in alignment with spiritual laws—basically, they can help us avoid making the mistakes so many of their people made and facing the suffering their civilization endured.

The Atlanteans who abused their spiritual powers or did not align their path with devotion and service have continued to work through the wheel of karma with incarnation after incarnation of learning to respect and honor the light. I believe many lightworkers here today have had Atlantean incarnations and are learning their lessons now.

The Halls of Amenti

Thoth has a spiritual retreat called the Halls of Amenti. This is a learning space that we can visit in the dream state and in meditation to access the wisdom of Thoth and receive activations to support us on our spiritual path.

Many spiritual seekers suggest that these halls are the sacred space that is hidden within the Great Pyramid of Egypt, but when I connect with the energy, I feel that they are in a completely different dimension. I believe that they are most likely a sacred temple of Atlantis that moved dimension before Atlantis ended.

The Hermetic Texts and the Emerald Tablet

The Hermetic texts are a series of Egyptian/Greek sacred texts from the second century or earlier. They are a series of dialogues between a teacher (Thoth/Hermes) and a student (the reader). The texts form the basis of Hermeticism, a spiritual tradition that brings together science and spirituality through the investigation of the cosmos, mind, and nature. They are based on the concept of alchemy, the art of turning lead into gold, or something that is leaden and heavy into a golden opportunity.

The most celebrated of the Hermetic texts is the *Emerald Tablet*. Legend has it that this "tablet" carved from a green gemstone (all green stones were referred to as emeralds in ancient times) was actually transported to Egypt after the fall of Atlantis and stored in a hidden temple under the Great Pyramid. Although this legend is widespread, the original source of the *Emerald Tablet* is unknown. The author signed off as "Hermes Trismegistus" and the text, which is made up of 14 passages, first appears in a book written sometime between the sixth and eighth centuries. One of its most influential statements is: "As above, so below," which has been adopted by magical circles the world over.

I have a replica of the *Emerald Tablet* that is written in Phoenician on translucent green resin. When I received this piece of "art," I had a deeper revelation about the *Emerald Tablet*. Although it reveals the interconnectedness of all things, I feel there is more to it than that, and reading and rereading it is a spiritual attunement that allows us to access higher knowledge. It's almost that through meditating on these powerful words, we invoke the cosmic light being that is Thoth and begin to have a deeper understanding of the universe and the part we play in it.

There are many translations of the *Emerald Tablet*, including some by leading figures in spirituality and philosophy such as Isaac Newton and Helena Blavatsky. Here's my personal version:

From the highest truth with complete certainty.

As above, so below. Working the miracles of One.

All things come from One.

Father in the sun. Mother in the moon.

Life-force is carried within. We are nourished by the Earth.

Power and intelligence are already perfected.

Separate the Earth from harm. Releasing without judgment.

Ascend with the greatest awareness from Earth to heaven. Unite with the One.

Align with the light of the whole universe and all uncertainty will fall away.

With this great knowing, all beings will be able to overcome all challenges.

This is the power of creation.

The divine plan is unfolding.

I am Hermes Trismegistus, wisdom-keeper of the universe.

My transmission of light is complete.

I believe ultimately the *Emerald Tablet* is about awakening the light within— it's the preparation guidelines for ascension, so that we can become great beacons of light upon the Earth. In the activation below you can welcome in all the principles it shares.

Working with Thoth

Working with Thoth helps you:

© accelerate your spiritual growth

© draw in the support of heaven and Earth

© overcome the challenges or setbacks of your ego

© form clear intentions

© transmute any darkness in your life into a golden opportunity

This activation allows you to receive a divine transmission from Thoth and call in the wisdom of the *Emerald Tablet* and the Halls of Amenti.

EMERALD TABLET ACTIVATION

Take a moment to center your energy. Rub your palms together to awaken your energy, then place them on your heart and connect with the stillness and wisdom within. You have an incredible teacher within and you are also a vessel that can bring light to the Earth. You have had many incarnations.

> *Thoth, great wisdom-keeper,*
> *Atlantean priest-king known by many names,*

Hermes, Mercury, Thrice-Great, thank you for transporting me through the stargate of my heart into the Halls of Amenti.

I am willing to receive your divine transmission and the activation of the Emerald Tablet.

Thank you for placing the wisdom codes of alchemy into my being, so that I may transmute all darkness and uncertainty into light.

I remember that all that is above is connected to all that is below.

I rejoice, knowing that all that is below is aligned to the heavens above.

I welcome the blessings of heaven and Earth into my heart.

Great sky father, bless me with your solar light.

Great mother of the moon, bless me with your lunar light.

Thoth, thank you for helping me align and connect with the life-force within.

Thank you for helping me recall the wisdom of lifetimes upon lifetimes.

I am willing to be guided by your magical light, knowing that you will help me follow my greatest calling, through my choices, with awareness and understanding.

Thank you for showing me how to remove harmful behaviors, people, and places from my world, so that I can be consumed by light, filled by grace, and live my purpose in a way that fulfils me.

I align with the powers of creation.

I trust that the divine plan is unfolding.

And so it is.

LADY VENUS

L ady Venus is an advanced cosmic being of ecstatic light dedicated
to helping us connect with divine wisdom. She is an interplanetary
representative of divine love and a bringer of the higher consciousness that
will support the ascension process for lightworkers and Planet Earth. She
is the twin flame of Sanat Kumara (*see p.230*) and she is often referred to as
Lady Venus Kumara, youthful or eternal Lady Venus. She is the overseer
of the planet Venus and the queen of the cosmic beings known as the
Venusians (*see p.257*).

Although she is a lesser known master than her twin flame, Lady Venus
has become better known and understood in recent times. She is said to
look like a young woman around the age of 16 with bright blonde hair and
human features similar to the quintessential Scandinavian girl. When I
clairvoyantly connect with her, I see a being made of brilliant light. She
looks somewhat extraterrestrial, but still has a humanoid stature. She is quite
tall and her aura is filled with gold and light pink. When she is present, the
air feels clean. Her piercing blue, almost lilac eyes are as bright as diamonds
shining in the midday sun. When I feel her energy come in, I feel my third
eye center activating and tingles around the crown of my head.

Venus

Astrologically, the planet Venus represents love, issues of the heart, sexuality, and vanity. Courtship, adoration, personal taste, personal values, and our relationship with possessions are all connected to its energy. When I called on Lady Venus to gain further understanding, I received clear information. It seems that our astrological view of Venus has become limited by the human mind and the human idea of potential. Venus is the planet that represents love—what we love and how we experience love on a human level—but if we are able to tap into the holy ideas about this planet, we'll be able to experience a lot more. This is what I received:

> *On a multi-dimensional level, Venus is the planet that represents your personal connection with the Divine. When you invoke the energy of Venus and the Venusian beings, you are able to be guided toward your own experience of divine love. Upon planet Earth, many of you human beings understand divine connection and the experience of the Divine through literature and study. The energy of Venus encourages you to harness your personal connection and understanding of the Divine within your own heart and at a higher heart level.*

So, Lady Venus helps us unlock our divine potential and experience the Divine on a heart level. We often try to connect with Source through what we've learnt from others. Lady Venus helps us go beyond the limitations that come with this. She helps us understand that learning about God and experiencing God are two completely different things.

If you've ever felt you're not good enough for God, Lady Venus is the Ascended Master to call upon. Maybe you've been brought up in a religious household or practiced a religion that has made you feel sinful or worthless.

This isn't what you were born to experience—you are here to experience divine love with all of your being.

The Venusians

The Venusians are advanced cosmic beings similar to angels who come from the planet Venus. They are our starry ancestors and are dedicated to helping us experience and embody divine love. When we call on them, they will come forth and guide us.

Just like angels, there are millions of Venusians and we can strike up a personal relationship with one, just as we can with a spiritual guide or guardian angel. The difference is, when the Venusian feels that their work with us is complete, they will move on to help others. This isn't because they are limited by time and space, more that they want to step back so that we can see how far we've come on the journey of awakening and ascension.

If you feel drawn to this information or you feel strongly connected to the stars or starpeople, there's a good chance that there are many extraterrestrial beings working with you at this time. It's important to say that there is no set way of working with or connecting with the Venusians, but they will contact you when necessary in dreams or meditation to share information that will support you on your journey.

Downloads, Upgrades, and Light Codes

Lady Venus helps us open up to downloads of spiritual information and insights that will be pivotal to our spiritual growth. The information can come through hearing messages or seeing visions, but can also be in the form of energetic upgrades.

In the past, during my personal meditations I would often feel that I'd been receiving information, but as I hadn't heard a message or clearly seen a next step, I'd be left wondering. When I asked for more information, my angel guides told me that I had been downloading light codes into my energy body that would support me in my work. Now I often see the download coming in. It might look like symbols or, if you've ever seen the movie *The Matrix*, those electronic codes that appear on the screen moving downward.

Ways to know you're receiving a download, upgrade, or light code:

© hearing random whistles, high-pitched tones, overtones, or otherworldly sounds, which are all frequency downloads coming in from heaven

© speaking in a language you don't know or understand

© hearing a guide speak to you in another language, most likely Light Language, a multi-dimensional high-frequency language that helps activate your energy body

© seeing the number 11:11—a clear sign that you are receiving support from Source

© feeling as though a message is coming through, even if you can't get a clear idea of what it is

© randomly drawing symbols in the air during energy work or while you're journaling, which is the human self-processing high-vibrational spiritual downloads

Often we can't fully comprehend a download when it is coming through. Of course we want to know exactly what it means or what it will do for us, but often these questions are coming from our ego. If you ever feel you do need to get to the bottom of information you've received, invite Lady Venus and the Venusians into your energy and ask them to help you unpack it.

Working with Lady Venus

Lady Venus can help you with:

© strengthening your spiritual connection

© opening up to a personal experience of Source/God

© creating alliances with star beings who can guide you personally

© downloading information that will support your growth

© increasing your "energetic bandwidth" to receive more on a spiritual level

Lady Venus can also help you go beyond any false and limiting ideas that have been placed upon you and that could be standing in the way of your growth or healing. If you are ready to shift them, say this prayer for 33 days:

Thank you, Lady Venus, for helping me rise above and beyond the limiting ideas, stories, or false narratives that have been placed in my heart and energy by others. I am now ready to break the bonds and chains that prevent me from rising high.

Thank you, Lady Venus, for guiding me out of my mind and back to my heart space so that I can have my own personal connection and experience of Source.

Thank you, Source energy, for allowing me to experience you directly.

I am ready to claim my worth.

Lady Venus's activation involves connecting to divine wisdom through our higher chakras and increasing the bandwidth to create an infra-red broadband-style connection.

INCREASING BANDWIDTH ACTIVATION

Center yourself with deep breathing.

Imagine your entire being radiating with ecstatic light.

Begin to chant internally, or out loud if you are comfortable with that, prolonging the sounds:

> *Lady, Venus (Laaaay deeee Veeeeeenus),*
>
> *Lady, Venus,*
>
> *Lady, Venus, thank you for wrapping my energy in your high-frequency light.*
>
> *I welcome your energetic upgrades into my field.*
>
> *Thank you for helping me make my own personal connection with Source.*
>
> *I am willing to have my own experience of divine love.*
>
> *I accept that I am a spark of the divine mind and align with this infinite intelligence now.*
>
> *Thank you for creating a visceral, embodied connection between my mind and the mind of Source.*
>
> *Through my crown chakra, Soul Star, and Stellar Gateway, I align, attune, and connect to ancient wisdom, starry wisdom, and the presence of light.*
>
> *Thank you for harnessing a powerful, inspired, and enhanced connection with the Divine.*
>
> *I welcome your blessings.*
>
> *I am willing to be led by your love.*

Thank you for helping me tap into my starry origins.

I welcome in the presence and leadership of the Venusians.

I am held by divine love.

I am replenished by divine love.

I am activated by divine love.

Thank you, Queen of Venus, lady of light, for blessing me with your presence.

I am aligned.

And so it is.

AWAKEN THE
MASTER WITHIN

Within you is a great light.

A light that will never go out.

A light that has the opportunity to shine whenever you face darkness.

Darkness is not the absence of light, but an invitation to express it.

An invitation to show up.

An invitation to remember.

An invitation to awaken.

Call that light from within.

Invite it to stand at the forefront of your mind and heart.

Let the light lead you.

Let the light guide you.

Let the light remind you who you truly are.

A cosmic being embodied.

A star in its next incarnation.

Ancient wisdom in human form.

The presence of love expressing itself.

A light that was born to shine.

Let the world experience your brilliance.

Feeling called to connect with the Masters of Ancient Wisdom is a sacred call. There's a reason for it. It isn't only because you're curious or you want to make a difference. It's because you're remembering something deeply sacred within. Something is happening deep inside you.

I believe that before you were in this body, before you were even human, you were cosmic energy, pure love, a source of light. You danced across the midnight sky, making the world a brighter place just by existing.

You used to be a star. You were given the opportunity to incarnate as a human being on planet Earth. You were given the space to come in and experience the lessons of life. It wasn't all mapped out for you, but before your first incarnation, you set the intention to remember who you truly were. It's likely that didn't happen, though, and that's why you've continued to incarnate and to experience more of the world.

You have been moving round the wheel of karma, living different lives, as different people, in different parts of the world. Each lifetime has felt like a lifetime, filled with lessons and experiences. But your soul has been expanding with every moment of love and loss. Expanding further with every lifetime.

This lifetime is different. You have remembered more than ever. You feel part of something greater—a universal life-force, a love that just keeps on loving. You know it's part of who you are and when you've completed this cycle, it's the place you'll return to. The strangest part is, you know that you've actually never left. Deep within your being, you are still one with everything that is, was, and ever will be. You are still that star dancing across the midnight sky, but you are now many other things and you have been many other people.

These are all reasons why you have a great master within you, an ancient, wise, and intelligent one. Sometimes they make themselves heard through your inner voice, but you can intentionally call them forth.

That's why the final activation of this book is to activate the master within. It's time to invite that ancient part of your being to lead. Let them help you integrate all you have learnt through all of your lifetimes. Let them help you awaken your spiritual gifts. Let them give you information on how you can resolve any past dramas, work through forgiveness, live purposefully, and feel the presence of your angels and guides.

The master within, just like the other masters, can't force their way into your world. They need an invitation. When you work through this activation, you issue that invitation and allow the masterful energy within to awaken and guide you.

Awaken the Master Within Activation

Dial into your breath.

Place your hands on your heart center.

Breathe deeply into your heart.

Connect with the tenderness there. Soften.

See yourself beyond this lifetime.

Visualize yourself as a star in the heart of the midnight sky.

Set the intention to see your true essence.

Know you are part of something greater.

Realize you're not alone.

Many angels and Divine Masters are gathering around you.

You are connected to and through the divine matrix.

Connect with the light within you.

Allow it to reveal itself to you.

Let its energy fill your human form.

Then say these activating words:

> *Awaken now, O great ancient one within, presence of light, sacred ebb and flow of life itself, resting at the heart of my being.*
>
> *I invite you to emerge.*
>
> *I welcome you at the forefront of my being.*
>
> *Thank you for leading me.*
>
> *Thank you for helping me remember the connectedness of all things.*
>
> *Thank you for allowing me to understand the great lessons of this incarnation.*
>
> *I am ready to surmount any previous karma and remember my true self.*
>
> *Like a great shining star in the midnight sky,*
>
> *I activate my infinite light.*
>
> *I activate my power to know.*
>
> *I activate the ancient master within.*
>
> *I return to the truest form of myself.*

Thank you, starlight self, for filling the cup of my being until I am
  overflowing.

I AM light.

I AM ancient wisdom embodied.

I remember.

And so it is.

Bring your hands to your heart space. Breathe and receive any guidance, images, or memories.

The master within has been activated. Now take them out into the world.

RECOMMENDED READING

Shirley Andrews, *Atlantis: Insights from a lost civilization*, Llewellyn Publications, 1997; AuthorHouse, 2018

—, *Lemuria and Atlantis: Studying the past to survive the future*, Llewellyn Publications, 2004

Helena Petrovna Blavatsky, *The Secret Doctrine*, 2 vols, Theosophical Publishing Company, 1888; Forgotten Books, 2008

Diana Cooper, *A Little Light on Ascension*, Findhorn Press, 1997

Judy Hall, *Crystal Skulls: Ancient tools for peace, knowledge and enlightenment*, Weiser Books, 2016

Tom Kenyon and Virginia Essene, *The Hathor Material: Messages from an ascended civilization*, S.E.E. Publishing Company, 1996; revised edition, 2012

Godfré Ray King, *Unveiled Mysteries*, 1934; Martino Fine Books, 2011; Start Publishing, 2012

—, *The Magic Presence*, 1935; Albatross Publishers, 2019

Drunvalo Melchizedek, *The Ancient Secret of the Flower of Life*, Light Technology, 1999

Robert Simmons, *The Book of Stones: Who they are and what they teach*, North Atlantic Books, 2005; revised edition, 2015

Robert K.G. Temple, *The Sirius Mystery*, St Martin's Press, 1976; revised edition, Inner Traditions, 1998

Hermes Trismegistus, *The Emerald Tablet of Hermes*, Merchant Books, 2013

Paramahansa Yogananda, *Autobiography of a Yogi*, The Philosophical Library, 1946; CreateSpace, 2015

—, *The Yoga of Jesus: Understanding the Hidden Teachings of the Gospels*, Self-Realization Fellowship, 2007

ABOUT THE AUTHOR

Bob Rafferty

Kyle Gray has had spiritual encounters from an early age. When he was just four years old, his grandmother's soul visited him from beyond the grave.

Growing up, Kyle always had an ability to hear, feel, and see what goes beyond the natural senses, and during his teens he discovered the power and love of the angels.

Now, Kyle is one of the world's leading angel experts who dedicates his life to helping others discover their spiritual gifts. He introduces the angels and spirituality in an accessible way to a modern audience and makes ancient spiritual knowledge relevant to today's reader.

Kyle is based in Glasgow, Scotland. He is the bestselling author of seven books and the co-creator of three oracle card decks.

 kylegrayuk

 @kylegrayuk

 @kylegrayuk

www.kylegray.co.uk

Certified Angel Guide

Online Video Course

Join one of today's most electrifying spiritual teachers and learn how to deepen your personal connection with the angels—and serve clients and friends as a Certified Angel Guide! In nine fun, informative lessons, **Kyle Gray** will share the tools, meditations, and exercises you need to supercharge your heavenly connection and lead an empowering and purpose-filled life.

You'll learn how to:

- Nurture your psychic gifts and unlock your spiritual potential
- Develop your angelic connection using powerful techniques
- Work with the archangels and ascended masters for guidance
- Connect people with angels through Angel Guide sessions
- Raise your vibration and channel angelic healing
- Create your own unique angelic communication toolkit

You're a lightworker and you're here to make a difference. Through training to become a Certified Angel Guide, not only will you nourish your relationship with your own angels, receive their messages, and recognize their daily presence; you'll also learn to facilitate a sacred space to help others connect with their angels, and share angelic healing, guidance, and protection with the world.

Learn more at hayhouse.co.uk

HAY HOUSE
online learning

Listen. Learn. Transform.

Listen to the audio version
of this book for FREE!

Connect with your soul, step into your purpose, and find joy with world-renowned authors and teachers—all in the palm of your hand. With the *Hay House Unlimited* Audio app, you can learn and grow in a way that fits your lifestyle . . . and your daily schedule.

With your membership, you can:

- Expand your consciousness, reclaim your purpose, deepen your connection with the Divine, and learn to love and trust yourself fully.

- Explore thousands of audiobooks, meditations, immersive learning programs, podcasts, and more.

- Access exclusive audios you won't find anywhere else.

- Experience completely unlimited listening. No credits. No limits. No kidding.

Try for FREE!

HAY HOUSE

Look within

Join the conversation about latest products,
events, exclusive offers and more.

f   Hay House

🐦   @HayHouseUK

📷   @hayhouseuk

🖤   healyourlife.com

We'd love to hear from you!